Who Benefits from Federal Education Dollars?

Who Benefits from Federal Education Dollars?

The Development of ESEA Title I Allocation Policy

James J. Vanecko
Nancy L. Ames

with

Francis X. Archambault, Jr.

Abt Books
Cambridge, Massachusetts

Library of Congress Cataloging in Publication Data

Vanecko, James J   1941-
    Who benefits from Federal education dollars?

    Bibliography: p.
    Includes index.
    1. Socially handicapped children—Education—
United States—Finance. 2. Federal aid to
education—United States. I. Ames, Nancy L.,
1945-   joint author. II. Archambault,
Francis X., 1944-   joint author.   III. Title.
LC4091.V36   371.96'7   79-55777
ISBN 0-89011-541-9

Contents

═══ Foreword ═══

This book deals with one of the most interesting and important demonstrations in education in the fourteen years since the federal government first began funding compensatory education programs through Title I of the Elementary and Secondary Education Act. Title I was sold to the Congress under the guise of the War on Poverty, even though it was aimed at providing not money but remedial education.

As the Congress began the reauthorizing process for Title I in 1973 and 1974 the key unresolved issue was whether or not low income must be maintained as the initial targeting threshold. In other words, would low achieving children not enrolled in low-income target schools continue to be denied the benefits of Title I? Despite my continued efforts in the 93rd Congress to define the target population in terms of educational rather than economic need, the 1974 Education Amendments (Public Law 93-380) maintained the low income threshold for service.

However, the same legislation did include a congressionally mandated study (Section 821) to be conducted by the fledgling National

Institute of Education. A major element of that study was an experimental program in not more than twenty school districts to explore alternative procedures for distributing Title I funds, including the use of measures of educational disadvantage. That provision led eventually to the selection of thirteen school districts, from Rhode Island to California, which used waivers of the law to try allocation approaches not then sanctioned. Most of the districts did in fact seek to utilize some measure of educational need in allocating funds.

This research effort was important because it was directly related to a number of policy concerns in both the legislative and executive branches. What the Congress learned from the study and its effect on policy formulation are set out in detail in the chapters that follow. Suffice it for me to note here that perhaps the most important result was that we discovered that school districts could in fact implement alternative allocation methods in an orderly and efficient manner and that many communities were anxious to break away from the federal school-targeting mechanisms that have shackled district initiative and creativeness in meeting the needs of deprived children. The demonstration succeeded in putting to rest many of the fears and myths that had surrounded the notion of a change in Title I allocation and targeting since I first began to push that notion by introducing legislation in the 93rd Congress.

Was the demonstration study effective in altering public policy? I believe it was. The postscript highlights the many changes that were in fact incorporated in the Education Amendments of 1978 (Public Law 95-561). Many of these changes were designed to give school districts more discretion in meeting the needs of their educationally disadvantaged students. Although no one study or factor was solely responsible for these changes in the law, it is my view that a good deal of the credit must go to the Section 821 study and specifically to the demonstration portion of that effort.

I hope that additional work along these lines will be carried out and that in another decade we will be able to look back and document the contribution that social science research has made to the evaluation of public policy. Although I have been in politics for most of my adult life, I have always operated on the premise that sound public policy was made not by politicians alone but through a combination of politics, facts, and simple logical thinking. In the past several years social science research has matured to the point where it has begun to have a significant impact on public policy. The Title I demonstration study is a prime example of that work at its best.

Albert H. Quie
Governor of Minnesota
Former Ranking Minority
Member of the Committee
on Education and Labor,
U.S. House of Representatives

══ Preface ══

This book represents the culmination of more than three years of collaborative research, during which numerous individuals assisted in the preparation of several technical reports, written and oral testimony to Congress, symposia, and journal articles. The collaboration has been intense, rewarding, and comprehensive. We hope that this final product will become a model for the communication and reporting of similar large-scale policy research. Perhaps such a hope is overreaching. However, we believe it is better to fall short, than not to try.

The demonstration study on which this book is largely based was originally conceived by the two ranking members of the House Subcommittee on Elementary, Secondary, and Vocational Education. These men disagreed on key issues related to the 1974 reauthorization of the Elementary and Secondary Education Act, but clearly recognized the need for knowledge in order to resolve their disagreements wisely. Thus, all who are concerned with federal education policy and its formulation owe a debt, as do we, to the Honorable

Carl Perkins, Chairman of the Committee on Education and Labor of the U.S. House of Representatives and to Albert Quie, then ranking minority member of that committee. Other subcommittee members were active architects of that compromise, as were the senate members of the conference committee: William Ford, John Braedamus, and Claiborne Pell.

An equal debt is owed to the chief staff members of the House: John Jennings, counsel to the subcommittee, and Christopher Cross, senior consultant to the minority. They were instrumental in formulating the National Institute of Education's (NIE) Study of Compensatory Education, of which this demonstration research was a part. They watched its progress closely, weaving its findings into the very fabric of the 1978 reauthorization.

A number of individuals at NIE were involved in the design and success of this collaborative research. The basic strategy for the study was developed by Paul Hill, the study director. The ultimate success of the overall study, its frequent citation in the legislative record, and its long-range impact on policy research should be credited to him. During the course of the research described in this book, he frequently proved to be a worthy adversary, a collegial critic, and a demanding client.

Iris Rotberg, as Paul Hill's deputy, took an active and helpful part in this research, as did other members of the NIE study team, Margot Nyitray, Gil Hoffman, Pierce Hammond, Donald Burnes, and Joy Frechtling.

The most constant and careful critic of our research and the person who was most responsible for seeing that all parts of the complicated machinery of the demonstration study were completed was Ann Milne. She was precise and demanding in her role as project monitor and was instrumental in the design, interpretation, and reporting of all phases of the demonstration research. Her contribution to the 1978 reauthorization may be seen in what we have come to call the Milne Amendment, Section 124(e) of Public Law 95-961.

This book would not exist without the enormous help we received from the school districts that participated in the demonstration. Thus, we owe a debt to the administrators, principals, teachers, parents, and school children of Adams County, Colorado; Alum Rock, California; Berkeley County, West Virginia; Boston, Massachusetts; Charlotte/Mecklenburg, North Carolina; Harrison County, West Virgina; Houston, Texas; Mesa, Arizona; Newport, Rhode Island; Racine, Wisconsin; Santa Fe, New Mexico; Winston-Salem/Forsyth, North Carolina; and Yonkers, New York.

Numerous individuals at Abt Associates contributed to the design and implementation of the research on which this book is based. The first person we should single out is Peter Miller, then Education Area manager. It was Peter who decided to respond to the request for proposals from NIE in the spring of 1975. Paul Summitt, John Doucette, and the senior author argued over issues of policy and research design, agreed finally, and wrote our preliminary approach to the study. The initial design described in that proposal provided the foundation on which much of the later analyses rested.

In addition to the proposal team, several other individuals contributed significantly in the early days of the project start-up. Donald Muse assisted with the overall sampling design; Walter Stellwagen helped formulate the overall research plan; Julia Shepard was instrumental in the design of the data collection plan; and Carol Lukas contributed to the development of several data collection instruments.

The success of any major research project depends on collecting information. The one person most responsible for the success of the data collection effort was Ruth Scheer. In a research project such as this one, busy school personnel are most likely to cooperate when they fully understand project goals and the methods of achieving them, and when those methods are precisely, reasonably, and practically designed and executed. Thanks to her able recruitment, training, and supervision, the data collection staff succeeded in gaining enthusiastic cooperation along with high response rates. In addition to Ruth, this staff included research coordinators located in each of the thirteen participating districts and two additional Cambridge-based field monitors—Marion Grogan and Ilana Rhodes. Finally, Lee Foster was tireless in his management of the distribution, collection, and handling of the thousands of questionnaires completed during the course of the three-year study.

The management and the complex data files for the study were directed by Glenn Takata, with assistance from Michael Duvos, David Poppe, and Ellen Lee. Also assisting with both data analysis and report preparation over the course of the project were Jaime Grubin, Rosamund Ladner, and Ennio Mingolla.

The administrative tasks involved in a study of this magnitude are many—budget monitoring, maintenance of study files, report production, assistance with internal and external communication, to name a few. This project was fortunate enough to have three extraordinarily fine administrative staff. Jacqueline Thomas was with the project from the beginning. As secretary and later as administrative assistant to the project director, her tenacity, spirit, and talent became the transmission that kept the machine rolling. The one staff member most responsible for production of the book was Mary-Ellen Perry. When Jacqueline was promoted to area administrative secretary, Mary-Ellen stepped in as project secretary to see that all our products were produced handsomely and efficiently. Finally, Claudia Kelly provided indispensable support to the field effort and the production staff. Her conscientious budget monitoring efforts during the last several months of the project were invaluable.

In addition to these project staff, three other persons deserve special recognition. David Budding and Robert Herriott were extremely helpful as technical reviewers, offering feedback and support under tremendous time pressure. Peter Desmond provided substantial editorial assistance on successive drafts.

Throughout the course of the project, a small number of research analysts were responsible for designing analyses and preparing technical reports. This book has been made possible by their high degree of professionalism and continuing dedication to the research endeavor. These persons are: Richard Ames, D. Catherine Baltzell, Nancy Brigham, Michael Hennessy, Jane Huseby Sjogren, Robert St. Pierre, and Glenn Takata. Each of these staff members, as well as Robert Silverstein of Long and Silverstein and David Boesel of Abt Associates, contributed substantially to the drafting of this book.

The drafts for each chapter were prepared as follows: introduction, chapter one, James Vanecko; chapter two, Robert Silverstein; chapter three, Nancy Ames; chapter four, Michael Hennessy and David Boesel; chapter five, Francis Archambault, Jr., D. Catherine Baltzell, and Jane Huseby Sjogren; chapter six, Ann Milne; chapter seven, Glenn Takata; chapter eight, Robert St. Pierre and Richard Ames; chapter nine, Nancy Brigham and D. Catherine Baltzell; and the postscript, Christopher Cross.

James J. Vanecko, *San Marino* and *Paris*
Nancy L. Ames, *Cambridge, Massachusetts*
Francis X. Archambault, Jr., *Storrs, Connecticut*

Introduction

Introduction

The education bill was part of a proliferating series of imaginative new federal programs aimed at declaring war on poverty and ignorance.

Richard Kluger[1]

One of the opening salvos in the "war on poverty and ignorance" was the passage of the Elementary and Secondary Education Act (ESEA) in 1965. Title I of ESEA has become the cornerstone of federal aid to our nation's elementary and secondary schools, providing financial assistance for compensatory instruction to educationally disadvantaged children in low-income areas. In 1978, with an appropriation of more than $2.7 billion, Title I provided financial assistance to 90 percent of the school districts in the country and served approximately 5.9 million children.

Since its enactment, Title I has occasioned numerous skirmishes on the legislative battlefield. The law has been amended nine times during its thirteen-year history, most recently in 1978. In spite of these conflicts, however, the legislation has remained remarkably

3

resilient. As described in *The Report on the Education Amendments of 1978, H.R. 15,* three essential features have characterized Title I since its inception:

> First, the central characteristic of the program is the way in which it directs funds to districts based on their numbers of low-income children, on the theory that poverty and low scholastic achievement are closely related. When Title I was first enacted in 1965, it was viewed as a response to a crisis in education, as evidenced by the alarming numbers of American youths and adults with basic educational deficiencies. In collecting evidence to determine how to deal with this crisis, the Committee [on Education and Labor] in 1965 observed a strong correlation between the levels of income and educational underachievement. The Committee was also concerned over findings of widespread poverty in the United States and findings that school districts with concentrations of poverty faced great difficulties in supporting even a basic educational program. Consequently, Title I appropriates funds to school districts on the basis of numbers of low-income children.
>
> Once funds reach the school building level, however, all children who are in need of compensatory education services are eligible for the program, regardless of family income. This is consistent with the second characteristic of Title I, its flexibility at the local level. Careful to safeguard States' and local districts' traditional control over education, the Congress deliberately avoided creating a legal framework which is unnecessarily restrictive with respect to the design or delivery of educational services. Rather, the Title I legislation left to local schools the decision as to what educational methods should be used in improving educational opportunities for deprived children.
>
> The only restrictions placed on the funds at the local level are meant to insure the third characteristic of Title I—that the Federal funds are categorical in nature and intended to provide specific types of children in specific areas with special services above and beyond those normally provided as part of the district's regular educational program. The Act contains various administrative, evaluation, and reporting requirements to guarantee that this is the case.[2]

This book is about Title I of ESEA. It addresses a simple question concerning distributive equity: *What* educational services reach *which* children as a result of this law? The theme of equity in the distribution of educational resources is repeated in interpreting the law, examining its implementation, and presenting the results of social scientific investigation. It is sometimes presented solo with simple

rhythms, as when we discuss legislative intent. At other times complicated harmonics and countervailing rhythms are necessary to describe
the complex implementation process. Always, we return to the basic
theme.

The intent of the law is simple—to help disadvantaged students.
The help comes in the form of money transferred from the U.S.
Treasury to state educational agencies, thence to local school districts,
where it pays for the provision of extra educational services, particularly extra instruction in reading.

Although the intent is simple, the law itself is fairly complicated.
It contains a set of rules designed to ensure that educationally disadvantaged students in low-income areas receive supplementary
services. Yet these rules also permit considerable latitude in the design
and delivery of compensatory educational services. Furthermore, the
rules are sufficiently ambiguous that federal, state, and local officials
often disagree over their interpretation.

Even if the law were more prescriptive and less ambiguous,
however, it would not fully determine what services reach which
students. Once a law is passed, it is necessary for an appropriate executive agency to promulgate regulations interpreting the law, to design
procedures for assisting state and local educational agencies, to establish mechanisms to assure that the law is enforced, and finally to distribute the funds. In the case of Title I, that agency is the U.S. Office
of Education (OE). Furthermore, the implementation process involves
not only the federal government, but also state educational agencies,
local school districts, and school administrators.

The implementation process is centered on funds allocation,
which consists of rules and decisions regarding eligibility for Title I
funds and services, actual distribution of funds to those eligible, and
use of allocated funds. A complicated series of steps involving all
levels of government ultimately determines what resources and services reach which children. At each step in the process inequities may
occur. Consider, for example, a hypothetical case in which two children live across the street from each other. Their families are minorities
and are poor, their housing is similar, and both children have a great
deal of difficulty learning to read. In short, they are students for
whom Title I of ESEA was intended. However, one student receives
help, and the other does not. Admittedly, this case is unusual, but
because such a thing can and does happen, we must determine how
and why. How else can we know how to prevent it from happening
too often?

Why does one student not receive aid while the other does? The simple problem is that the allocation of resources within the Title I program takes place through a process which identifies some schools (those with above-average concentrations of students from low-income families) as eligible to receive Title I benefits and others as not eligible. Schools have attendance area boundaries that frequently go down the middle of a street. In this example the two students attend different schools. One school has a slightly higher concentration of students from poor families than the other. The first school thus becomes eligible to receive Title I benefits and the second does not, meaning that the student attending the first school may receive benefits and the student attending the second may not.

This is a simple problem of inequity which is inherent in the Title I legislation. More complicated problems arise in the implementation of the law. Both the simple and complicated problems must be considered in any attempt to eliminate inequity within the program.

Two characteristics of students are involved in addressing the problem of distributive equity. First, because Title I of ESEA is intended to alleviate the problems of poverty, the financial situation of students' families is important. Second, because Title I is intended to help students who have difficulty in school, especially in reading, students' educational achievement is important.

A significant aspect of the creation of Title I was the recognition that these two forms of disadvantage are related. Students whose families are poor are more likely to have difficulty reading than students whose families are financially secure. The complicated funds allocation system addresses both kinds of disadvantage at various steps in the process. However, the two are not perfectly related by any means. Not all students from poor families have difficulty reading, and not all students who have difficulty reading are from poor families.

Four types of students are depicted in the figure below. Each cell in that figure has been designated with two initials. The first is either A for adequate income or I for inadequate income. The second initial is either S for slow progress in reading or R for rapid progress in reading. The majority of students are in the AR cell (adequate income and rapid progress in reading). The next largest group includes those students in the IS cell (inadequate income and slow progress in reading). The students in the AR cell are the least likely to receive Title I services. Thus, in general the intent of the Title I legislation is fulfilled. However, there are more complicated problems which we can outline by classifying students in this way.

CLASSIFICATION OF STUDENTS

	SLOW PROGRESS	RAPID PROGRESS
FAMILY INCOME ADEQUATE	AS	AR
FAMILY INCOME INADEQUATE	IS	IR

The simple problem described above is one in which two students are both in the IS cell but, by virtue of school attendance, one receives services and the other does not. A closely related problem arises when eligible schools or programs or classrooms receive different amounts of resources: both students in the IS cell receive services but one student receives more extensive or better quality services than the other.

This situation arises in the hypothetical school district shown in the figure below. There are three schools in this district: the Carl Perkins School, the Francis Keppel School, and the Edith Green School. Each has 100 students. The four types of students are in different proportions in each school, as indicated in the figure. As a result of the different student body compositions, the Carl Perkins School and the Francis Keppel School are eligible to receive Title I resources while the Edith Green School is not eligible. In addition, funds are allocated in a relatively simple manner. The pricing unit is half the time of a reading specialist who is paid $13,500 a year. Since the Carl Perkins School has a much larger number of students whose reading progress is slow, this school receives two half-time reading specialists while the Francis Keppel School receives one. Because a teacher can handle fifty students in half a day, fifty students receive reading instruction in this school.

Thus, what we have described appears to be a relatively simple and fair system for allocating Title I resources. Unfortunately the results of these procedures are not so obviously fair, nor are they simple. We have repeated here the first problem: the IS student who lives in the attendance area of the Edith Green School does not receive help.

EDUCATIONAL SERVICES RECEIVED IN THREE SCHOOLS
LOCATED IN ONE DISTRICT

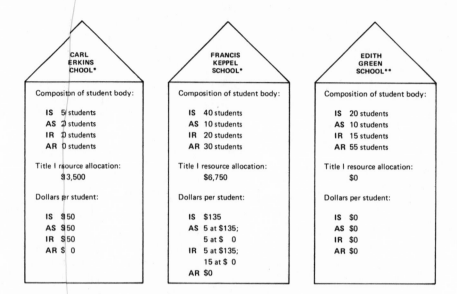

CARL
PERKINS
SCHOOL*

Composition of student body:

  IS 5 students
  AS 2 students
  IR 0 students
  AR 0 students

Title I resource allocation:
    $3,500

Dollars per student:

  IS $50
  AS $50
  IR $50
  AR $ 0

FRANCIS
KEPPEL
SCHOOL*

Composition of student body:

  IS 40 students
  AS 10 students
  IR 20 students
  AR 30 students

Title I resource allocation:
    $6,750

Dollars per student:

  IS $135
  AS 5 at $135;
       5 at $ 0
  IR 5 at $135;
      15 at $ 0
  AR $0

EDITH
GREEN
SCHOOL**

Composition of student body:

  IS 20 students
  AS 10 students
  IR 15 students
  AR 55 students

Title I resource allocation:
    $0

Dollars per student:

  IS $0
  AS $0
  IR $0
  AR $0

*This school is eligible for Title I services because it has an above-average proportion of students whose families are poor.
**This school is not eligible for Title I.

KEY

IS = Inadequate family income, slow progress
AS = Adequate family income, slow progress
IR = Inadequate family income, rapid progress
AR = Adequate family income, rapid progress

Moreover, if we assume that the process of identifying the students with reading problems is not perfect, it is possible that students are selected whose family income is inadequate and who appear to have reading problems but really do not (that is, the IR). The result is that some students in the Francis Keppel School who ought to receive reading instruction because of their slow progress do not. However, in the Carl Perkins School, because there really are not as many students in need of help as there is help available, all the students who actually need help, as well as some who may not, receive it.

Another result of these apparently simple procedures is that students in the Carl Perkins School either receive more instruction time or receive instruction in smaller groups than do the students in the

Francis Keppel School. The monetary equivalent of this difference is that for every student who is at all eligible for Title I help in the Carl Perkins School approximately $150 of resources is available. In the Francis Keppel School approximately $135 is available per student, and that figure does not account for every student who might be eligible.

Thus, with this hypothetical example we have illustrated three of the key problems of equity in the implementation of Title I of ESEA. First, some students who need services cannot get them because their school is not eligible to receive Title I. In many cases, this is due to the somewhat arbitrary boundaries of school attendance areas. Second, some students who need help cannot get it because there is not enough help to go around in their school and/or because of in-accurate identification procedures. Third, some students who need as much help as other students do not get as much because of the way the services are distributed from one school to another. These are simple versions of some complicated problems in the allocation of resources under Title I.

The remainder of this book provides a detailed documentation and analysis of both the typical results of funds allocation procedures and the exceptions. We will return again and again to the issue of dis-tributive equity—what quantity and quality of services are being delivered to what types of students.

As we address that issue, three different stories unfold. The first is the story of how the law was developed and modified. The second is the story of implementation: how regulations and guidelines, to-gether with administrative procedures, determine the manner in which educational services are delivered. The third is the story of alternatives to the law which were formulated and tested in several school districts.

Research on Title I of ESEA is not new; it has been studied from its inception in 1965. In fact, this law was one of the first to require objective evaluation of its impact, largely due to the influence of Robert F. Kennedy. He and his advisors shared a commitment to ex-tending the process by which legislation and resulting programs are scrutinized.

Social scientists undertook a wide variety of evaluations of Title I from 1965 to 1974. The evaluations were designed to be objective and scientific. The results—perhaps because of very high expectations—were mixed and disappointing. Legislators felt that they did not have adequate information to judge whether Title I worked or not. They also felt that the research undertaken up to 1974 did not indicate whether there were better alternatives for fulfilling the intent of the law.

This book describes research conducted from 1975 to 1978 in response to Congressional demand for better information. It tells why that research was undertaken, the results of the research, and implications for federal policy. Perhaps most important, the book tells how the research findings influenced the legislative decisions that were made in 1978. The facts are summarized in the report of the House Committee on Education and Labor:

> Early evaluations of the Title I program were critical of program administration and effectiveness; however, these evaluations were not nationally uniform and for the most part addressed only one of the purposes of the legislation, promoting students' academic development.
>
> When Congress last extended Title I in 1974 considerable debate occurred over whether or not Title I was achieving its objectives and this debate was only exacerbated by the lack of conclusive research findings.
>
> Feeling the need for this information to make important decisions in any future sets of amendments, Congress directed the National Institute of Education to conduct a comprehensive three-year study of Title I in the Education Amendments of 1974, P.L. 93-380. In order to insure that an adequate and objective report be presented, Congress stipulated that $5 million for each of the next three years be provided for the study out of the regular Title I appropriations and that NIE be the agency responsible for the evaluation.
>
> ...the findings of the NIE study were transmitted to Congress by September 30, 1977. The committee has found the quality of the research by NIE to be excellent and has consequently relied upon these reports in formulating amendments to Title I.[3]

One of the largest projects undertaken within the National Institute of Education (NIE) study was an examination of alternative policies and methods for allocating Title I resources *within* school districts. Thirteen school districts adopted alternative allocation procedures under waivers of federal regulations and Abt Associates Inc. examined how those changes affected what educational services reach which children. The results of that project along with some of the other research supported by NIE provide most of the data utilized in this book.

The discussion of equity in allocation is divided into two parts. Part one describes Title I prior to the passage of the Education Amendments of 1978. We trace the history of the legislation and high-

light the issues which have generated extensive public debate and resulted in numerous revisions of the law. We also outline the rules
governing the allocation of Title I funds, as well as the formal and
informal mechanisms designed to ensure that the rules are followed.
Finally, we consider the extent to which the rules, as administered
by federal and state agencies and implemented by local school districts, achieve the equity goals of the Title I legislation.

Part two examines alternatives to the rules that have governed
distribution of Title I funds for more than a decade. Using data from
the thirteen school districts which participated in the demonstration,
we describe the impact of alternative allocation policies on distributive equity.

We conclude with a postscript on the way in which the research
has influenced federal policy and the remaining legislative and administrative issues which must be resolved in the next few years.

Title I of ESEA is the most important federal aid program for
public schools in the United States. Our analysis of it has implications
for other federal programs, many of which are not fully funded and
thus cannot meet the needs of all the people they might serve. Such
programs are also guided by a set of rules which have intended beneficial effects and unintended inequitable consequences. This examination of Title I shows how social scientific evidence can be produced,
communicated, and used to modify and improve the law.

Notes

1. Richard Kluger, *Simple Justice* (New York: Alfred A. Knopf, 1976).

2. Committee on Education and Labor, U.S. House of Representatives, 95th
Congress, 2nd Session, *Report on the Education Amendments of 1978,
H.R. 15* (Washington, D.C.: House of Representatives, May 11, 1978), p. 4.

3. Ibid., p. 5.

PART ONE

How It Was

1

The History of
ESEA Title I

The Elementary and Secondary Education Act of 1965 was born in the transition from the Kennedy administration to the Johnson administration. Conceived by Robert Kennedy and initially proposed to Congress by John Kennedy, it was through the cooperative midwifery of Lyndon Johnson and Congressman Carl Perkins that the bill finally became law.[1]

ISSUES SURROUNDING THE ENACTMENT OF ESEA

ESEA was one of several legislative initiatives in the mid-1960s which originated in the emerging social policy technocracy of the major universities and the populist equalitarian politics of Lyndon Johnson. These initiatives were designed to mobilize anticipated federal surpluses in order to provide the poor with services not being offered by local governments. Program accountability and evaluation were emphasized in the legislation in an effort to render programs that would be self-corrective. With respect to ESEA, each of these characteristics entailed a set of political-philosophical issues which have been debated throughout the history of the legislation.

ESEA was enacted in response to a perceived crisis in education, as evidenced by the large numbers of youths and adults with basic educational deficiencies. The nation's school districts were thought to be unable (because of their limited taxing powers and the taxpayers' disposition) to generate enough resources to improve the academic performance of school children, and to encourage students to continue their education. ESEA was drafted in order to add a large sum of federal money to the resources already available to school districts, in the belief that the federal government could launch efficient educational reform.

Passage of the act represented the culmination of many pressures to increase federal involvement in education. From the end of World War II to 1965, demographic and socioeconomic changes placed demands on the U.S. educational system, and these in turn brought cries for federal assistance. The population growth of the postwar era created a need for new facilities and teachers, yet education had to compete with other demands for state and local assistance. The federal government responded to individual crises by passing specific pieces of legislation: the GI bill was enacted on behalf of returning veterans and the National Defense Education Act was passed in the wake of Sputnik. However, no comprehensive or coherent federal policy existed. Thus, with the signing into law of ESEA, the federal government committed itself for the first time to a significant role in education.

Passage of ESEA did not occur without intense debate. Opponents sought to limit what they perceived to be federal interference in local government. They argued that the U.S. Constitution assigned responsibility for education to the states, thus precluding federal involvement. Beneath this appeal to the Constitution, however, lay other concerns. Some feared that an expanded federal role in education would lead to even greater expenditures when new constituencies were organized. Others believed that federal involvement would destroy the diversity of the educational system and lead to a national, ideologically uniform curriculum. Also, opponents cited the ineptitude of the federal bureaucracy as reason enough for avoiding greater federal involvement in education.

The debate over federal involvement which raged during these early years has evolved to the point where the complexity of intergovernmental relations is now assumed. As Bailey and Mosher describe it:

> Quality and quantity of opportunity in education have become matters of national concern. All levels of government, and a variety of branches and agencies at each level, are now deeply involved in a complex and

uneasy partnership whose collective aims are transforming educational priorities and methods. Education, like so many other governmental services, has now become involved in a "marble cake," not a "layer cake," of federalism.[2]

The issue now debated in not *whether* but *how* the federal government should be involved in local education.

At the time the original legislation was passed, Congress was faced with two basic choices. It could alleviate fears that the federal government would take over schooling by providing general aid to school districts with few or no strings attached. Or, it could ensure that those most in need of assistance received it by targeting the funds on special populations and controlling the use of these funds tightly. Title I of ESEA represented a compromise. The federal government offered financial relief to school districts and allowed the districts some flexibility in using funds; however, in order to maximize the impact of those dollars, help was concentrated on selected school districts, schools, and students.

Title I was thus designed to focus resources on those considered to be most in need (and most deprived) of them. However, determining which groups are most in need and ascertaining whether Title I is reaching them have been recurring concerns. Debates over these issues have resulted in nine different amendments to the law, most recently in 1978. At issue are the mechanisms requiring school districts to channel resources so that educational opportunity is equalized.

In collecting evidence to determine how to deal with the perceived crises in education, Congress observed a strong correlation between level of income and educational disadvantage. Also, analyses suggested that educational opportunity resulting from local initiatives was unequal for two reasons. First, the concentration of poverty in specific areas and among specific groups created barriers between the education provided and the ability to learn; that is, children in "poverty-impacted" schools were seen as being in need of special services. Second, these same schools, which were often in decaying neighborhoods, typically received fewer resources—less experienced staff and poorer facilities and equipment—than their wealthier counterparts. Thus, the very schools which were deemed in need of additional resources were being denied even a basic level of support. In response to these findings, Title I required allocation to districts and schools with high concentrations of *poverty* and to students who were *educationally* disadvantaged within those schools.

The question that has been debated since the passage of Title I is whether concentrations of poverty actually create educational barriers which need to be redressed through federal government intervention, or whether the real barrier is simply one of educational disadvantage regardless of income. More specifically, the debate centers on whether funds should be distributed on the basis of measures of poverty or educational disadvantage (for example, test scores). This debate has concerned every level of the allocation process—federal to state, state to district, district to school and program, school and program to student. A corollary issue is whether the Title I legislation is meant to redress educational disadvantage, whatever the source, or whether it is intended only to redress educational disadvantage resulting from poverty (and discrimination, as some would argue). In terms of programs, the question is: What legislation, regulations, guidelines, or criteria must be developed and implemented to achieve distributive equity in the provision of educational opportunity?

The third characteristic—the effort to establish accountability and ensure adequate evaluation—has probably received more legislative attention through Title I than it has in any of the other Great Society programs for two reasons. First, unlike public welfare and unemployment compensation, Title I is not a direct cash assistance program which can be assessed simply in terms of the fact that the service is provided. Rather, it is a multiservice program in which the resources provided are only means to the achievement of established goals. Second, unlike the many multiservice programs which have set goals that are diffuse, ambiguous, competing, and sometimes even conflicting (thus impossible to measure, despite the good intentions of the legislative sponsors), the Title I goals of improving students' test scores seems to invite more straightforward measurement and evaluation.

Title I generated a serious attempt to organize accountability and evaluation efforts. Each step of the developmental process entailed elaboration of the complex implications of program goals and debate about the goals themselves. One question led to another: Do the programs account for the funds properly? Do districts spend the funds as they say they spend them? Is district behavior consistent with the legislative intent? Is district allocation of funds effective? Are the benefits of Title I programs, if any, worth the costs? How and why are programs effective? To answer each succeeding question required more sophisticated, sometimes better, and sometimes new research technology.

The legislative development of Title I of ESEA and the public debate surrounding it have frequently focused on these and other issues of accountability and evaluation. However, the legislative process has not resulted in legislation or regulations which address these questions independently. Instead, they are addressed through a blend of monitoring, auditing, needs assessment, and program evaluation procedures.[3] While most of those concerned about the future of Title I believe that the various mechanisms of accountability and evaluation should be continued, there is disagreement about how they should be organized and implemented.

Thus, the issues surrounding Title I of ESEA were only partially resolved with the passage of the act in 1965. The statutory objectives have evolved during the ensuing years of implementation, and corollary issues have evolved with them. This evolution can be described in terms of three stages in the development of Title I policy.

1965-1970: PROGRAM DEVELOPMENT AND ELABORATION

During the first stage, which lasted roughly from 1965 to 1970, Title I was implemented in school districts across the country, regulations and guidelines were developed, and a basic constituency for the program was built. The parameters of the debate over Title I policy were and still are determined by much of the rule making which occurred during this period. Furthermore, many local practices, some of which represented unplanned consequences of the laws and rules, were initiated during these early years.

Decisions made during this stage were dominated by the liberal wing of the Democratic Party. This included liberal members of Congress, especially the House Education and Labor Committee; allies of the civil rights movement; academic supporters of the Democratic Party and their colleagues in the Johnson administration; and the newly emerging cadre of black elected officials. These groups demanded and obtained tighter federal control of state and local use of federal dollars, with funds targeted strictly on educationally disadvantaged students in low-income areas. Although some compromises were made in recognition of the problems school administrators faced in implementing federal programs, the tightening of federal control was clear and consistent.

One of the first steps taken toward ensuring increased accountability was the requirement that reports on successful projects and effective methods for implementing Title I be produced. Congress also required "comparability": the level of basic resources in Title I schools—before Title I funds are added—must be equivalent to that of other schools in the district. In order to guarantee that the services paid for by federal money supplement those that would otherwise be provided to disadvantaged students, "supplement-not-supplant" provisions were also formulated during this period. Districts were required to convince Title I officials that the services provided to disadvantaged students would not have been provided without Title I funding. Finally, the notion of "maintenance of effort" emerged as a significant feature of Title I. By preventing districts from reducing their overall expenditures upon receipt of Title I funding, the maintenance-of-effort requirement provided yet another test of whether or not Title I services were truly additive.

In addition to these changes, parental involvement in Title I was also legislated and, by implication, parental demand for accountability. School districts were required to have parent advisory councils that would review the program, review applications for funding, and otherwise advise district Title I administrators. Also, the formula for distributing the national appropriation became more sophisticated during this time period. General and specific measures of poverty were combined, and state educational expenditures were added to the formula.

Federal funding increased during this early phase and a diverse group of advocates emerged. Parents of children who were served by the program became strong advocates, along with state and local superintendents and their boards. Civil rights organizations and their allies constituted another advocacy group. Finally, state and local Title I administrators became advocates and, by explaining the program to others, built additional citizen support.

By the end of the 1960s many of the important features of the program had been developed. Furthermore, a coalition of supporters had been established. It was not formal and there were differences which could split it. But, unlike other Great Society programs (for example, the Community Action Program), the constituency for Title I was sufficiently large and well organized that extinction at the hands of opponents was not a possibility.

1971-1974: QUESTIONING THE NATURE OF THE PROGRAM AND WHO SHOULD BENEFIT FROM IT

There was an obvious secular change in the early 1970s. Richard Nixon, having replaced Lyndon Johnson in 1968, began to turn his attention to domestic affairs as the war in Viet Nam wound down. The Department of Health, Education, and Welfare (HEW) was under new leadership. Thus, a new set of actors became influential, individuals who had not been involved in the developments of the mid-1960s and who were not wedded to current policies and practices.

Coincident with the change in leadership at HEW, the first major results of the evaluation required by law became available.[4] Although the results of this evaluation were interpreted differently by different actors, none found it possible to interpret Title I as an unqualified success. Title I also came under scrutiny from a number of other sources. Several criticisms of the program emerged:

School districts that were in financial straits viewed Title I as "general aid" and spent it accordingly, failing to provide truly compensatory services.

Monitoring by OE and the state educational agencies was inadequate.

Districts attempted to serve too many students at once and resources were spread too thin.

Title I resources merely substituted for state compensatory funds that would otherwise have been made available.

Guidelines and regulations were too restrictive.

Most of the compensatory programs did not work, and the research necessary to find out which ones were successful had not been performed.

The correlation between poverty and educational performance had been misinterpreted and misapplied.

Many of the concerns most important for allocation policy were voiced in an influential critique of Title I by Ruby Martin and Phyllis McClure.[5] The authors' contention that the law was being violated led to the formation of a high-level Title I task force. In its report, *New Directions for Compensatory Education,* the task force made six "urgent" recommendations, including a minimum expenditure of $150 per Title I-eligible student.[6] It was also suggested that a concentration of about $300 per student might be necessary to provide "appreciable impact."

At the same time an important policy analysis was completed by the Assistant Secretary for Planning and Evaluation, Constantine Menges.[7] He argued that compensatory education does work, but only if expenditures for it are $300 per student or greater. Menges discounted early evaluations on the grounds that they investigated only programs that spent less than that amount or they studied a mixture of programs, some of which spent more and some of which spent less.

The change in political leadership, coupled with the disappointing evaluation results and widespread criticism, provoked intensive questioning of the direction and efficacy of the Title I program. In fact, Title I might have been seriously weakened had it not been for another significant development in education during the early 1970s—the movement of desegregation north. Although the Nixon administration did not generally favor increased federal involvement in education, in the sensitive political climate of the 1972 election year, compensatory education represented a large carrot to be held out to school districts faced with desegregation. The above-mentioned policy analysis also played into the congressional politics of the situation. Although Menges concluded that evaluation results were ambiguous, he also called for more intensive federal support. As a result, Title I was not only reauthorized but expanded, as a companion to the new desegregation assistance authorization, the Emergency School Aid Act (ESAA).

While funding for Title I was thus secured, the direction of the program was not. Since its enactment in 1965, many had questioned whether Title I was an educational or a poverty program. In fact, in a national survey of school administrators conducted in May 1966, approximately 70 percent of the respondents stated that Title I funds should *not* be allocated on the basis of poverty.[8]

In the early 1970s this debate was revived as new evidence brought to light the complicated relationship between income level and educational achievement. Given the less-than-perfect correlation between the two, some argued that a sizable proportion of educationally disadvantaged students were being excluded from the program simply because they did not attend schools in low-income areas.

Albert Quie, the ranking Republican on the House Committee on Education and Labor at the time, led the House debate. He argued that since Title I is designed to provide educational services, it is essential to determine how it can best be targeted on the students who need the program most—the educationally disadvantaged. Congressman Quie suggested that Title I resources be distributed to states, counties, districts, and schools based on the number of children unable to perform adequately on achievement tests.

This second stage in the history of Title I culminated in the passage of the Education Amendments of 1974. The act included major changes in the formula for allocating funds to states and counties, but changes in the rules governing local school districts were minimal. A decision regarding the adoption of achievement-based allocation procedures was deferred, pending scientific investigation. Lacking clear evidence of the effectiveness of Title I and disagreeing over its future course, Congress instead called for extensive research and evaluation of the program by both the U.S. Office of Education (OE) and the National Institute of Education.

1974-1978: TESTING ALTERNATIVES AND MODIFYING THE LAW

The Education Amendments of 1974 authorized NIE to conduct a major study of compensatory education and examine several of the critical issues raised during the 1974 deliberations. In an unusual move, Congress explicitly precluded the study results from undergoing clearance by the Secretary of Health, Education, and Welfare in order to prevent the executive with most at stake, and implicitly Title I program staff, from placing political interpretations on the results.

Specifically, NIE was mandated to:

examine the fundamental purpose and effectiveness of compensatory education programs;

analyze ways of identifying children in greatest need of compensatory education;

consider alternative ways of meeting these children's needs; and

consider the feasibility, costs, and consequences of alternative ways of distributing compensatory education funds.

The demonstration component of the research, on which much of this book is based, was designed in response to the last of these mandates. Two provisions in the law refer to the demonstration. The first [Section 821(a)(5)] states that the NIE study should include:

...not more than 20 experimental programs, which shall be reasonably geographically representative, to be administered by the Institute, in cases where the Institute determines that such experimental programs are

necessary ... the Commissioner of Education is authorized, notwithstanding any provision of Title I of the Elementary and Secondary Education Act of 1965, at the request of the Institute, to approve the use
of grants which educational agencies are eligible to receive under such
Title I (in cases where the agency eligible for such grant agrees to such
use) in order to carry out such experimental programs.

The second reference is contained in Section 150 of the statute, which
states:

For any fiscal year not more than 20 local educational agencies selected
for the purpose of 821(a)(5) of the Educational Amendments of 1974
may elect, with the approval of the district-wide parent advisory council which is required to be established under Section 141(a)(14) of this
title, to allocate funds received from payments under this title on the
basis of a method or combination of methods other than the method
provided under Section 141(2)(14)(A). Any method selected pursuant
to this section shall be so designed and administered as to be free from
racial or cultural discrimination.

The wording of Sections 821 and 150, as well as the concerns
embodied in the history of those provisions, gave NIE clear instructions about how the demonstrations should be conducted. Participa-
ing districts would be free to allocate their funds in a manner other
than that ordinarily required by statute. They would identify children in "need," design services to meet this need, and choose alternative methods for distributing funds to support the services. Proposed
projects would require the approval of the district parent advisory
council. Finally, the method of allocation elected by each district
would, at the request of NIE, be approved by the U.S. Commissioner
of Education, "notwithstanding any provision of Title I of the Elementary and Secondary Act of 1965"—in other words, compliance
with certain statutory and regulatory provisions of Title I would be
waived.

A number of school districts responded to NIE's Request for Proposals to participate in the demonstration. NIE selected sixteen of
these districts to participate during the initial planning year. Proposals
were reviewed on the basis of three criteria: (1) quality, including
policy relevance of the proposed allocation method; (2) geographical
representation; and (3) approval by the parent advisory council.

Although selection was not designed to be random or to result in
a fully representative group of school districts, the sixteen districts
selected were nevertheless diverse. They varied in size, geographical
location, the urban or rural character of the communities they en-
compassed, and the proportions of their poor and minority group

populations. Moreover, a comparison of their demographic characteristics with those of a nationally representative sample of districts indicated few differences. They were, however, atypical in one respect: several had recently undergone either court-ordered or voluntary desegregation.

Of the sixteen districts which participated in the demonstration during the planning year, thirteen chose to submit implementation plans:[9]

Adams County #12, Colorado	Mesa, Arizona
Alum Rock, California	Newport, Rhode Island
Berkeley County, West Virginia	Racine, Wisconsin
Boston, Massachusetts	Santa Fe, New Mexico
Charlotte/Mecklenburg, North Carolina	Winston-Salem/Forsyth, North Carolina
Harrison County, West Virginia	Yonkers, New York
Houston, Texas	

NIE approved all thirteen plans, and Title I regulations were waived so that the districts could use alternative allocation methods during the 1976-77 and 1977-78 school years.

Findings from the demonstration, as well as from the other NIE and OE studies mandated by law, became the focus of legislative debate in the deliberations preceding passage of the Education Amendments of 1978. Ironically, by carefully insulating NIE from political influence, Congress had set the stage for intense political use of the evaluation findings. Paul Hill, the director of the NIE study, treated Congress as the client and information as its need. He explicitly precluded any interpretations or recommendations from being included in the research reports prepared for Congress. Thus, Congress was free to draw its own conclusions from the findings, conclusions which varied considerably based on political and philosophical orientations. Nevertheless, researchers were called to testify and offer their interpretations; results were scrutinized and debated. Ultimately, Congress was to cite the study as the most comprehensive and useful undertaken by the federal government.

As a result, in 1978 the law underwent greater revision than had ever been attempted before. Congress decided that the question of whether the program works educationally could not be answered, but that by the next reauthorization, in 1983, the answers ought to be ready. However, that goes beyond the perspective of this book, which is focused on the period from 1975 to 1978 and the study of Title I that the U.S. Congress mandated in 1974.

Notes

1. For informative accounts of the issues in the early 1960s and their resolution in 1965, see Philip Meranto, *The Politics of Federal Aid to Education in 1965: A Study in Political Innovation* (Syracuse, N.Y.: Syracuse University Press, 1967); and Stephen K. Bailey and Edith K. Mosher, *ESEA: The Office of Education Administers a Law* (Syracuse: Syracuse University Press, 1968).

2. Bailey and Mosher, *ESEA: The Office of Education Administers a Law*, p. 2.

3. For discussions of evaluation in the Title I program, see Richard L. Fairley, "Accountability's New Tool," *American Education* 8 (June 1972): 33-35; Kathryn A. Hecht, "Five Years of Title I Federal Evaluation," paper presented at the annual meeting of the American Educational Research Association, Chicago, April 1972; Milbrey Wallin McLaughlin, *Evaluation and Reform: The Elementary and Secondary Education Act of 1965, Title I* (Santa Monica, Calif.: Rand Corporation, January 1974); and Jerome T. Murphy, "Title I of ESEA: The Politics of Implementing Federal Education Reform," *Harvard Educational Review* 41 (February 1971): 35-63.

4. M.J. Wargo et al., "ESEA Title I: A Re-analysis and Synthesis of Evaluation Data from Fiscal Year 1965 Through 1970" (Palo Alto, Calif.: American Institute for Research, 1972).

5. Ruby Martin and Phyllis McClure, *Title I of ESEA: Is It Helping Poor Children?* (Washington, D.C.: Washington Research Project, NAACP Legal Defense and Educational Fund, 1970).

6. *New Directions for Compensatory Education,* report of the Title I Task Force to the Secretary of Health, Education, and Welfare (January 1971). Although originally confidential, this report is now available to the public under the Freedom of Information Act.

7. Office of the Assistant Secretary for Planning and Evaluation, *The Effectiveness of Compensatory Education: Summary and Review of Evidence* (Washington, D.C.: U.S. Department of Health, Education, and Welfare, April 20, 1972).

8. Bailey and Mosher, *ESEA: The Office of Education Administers a Law*.

9. The three districts which chose not to continue were Freeport, New York; Oklahoma City, Oklahoma; and Wichita, Kansas. Hereafter Charlotte/Mecklenburg and Winston-Salem/Forsyth will be referred to as Charlotte and Winston-Salem respectively.

===== 2 =====

The Title I
Legal Framework

As noted in chapter one, Title I of ESEA is not a simple grant-in-aid program that provides general funding to states and local school districts. Instead, Title I provides monies to school districts to meet the special educational needs of educationally deprived children living in areas with high concentrations of children from low-income families. Local school districts are responsible for actually designing Title I programs and providing compensatory educational services to the intended program beneficiaries. An application for funding, which is submitted to the state educational agency for approval, must contain assurances or demonstrate that the district will comply with particular Title I requirements.[1] The statutory basis for these requirements can be found in the following congressional declaration of policy:

> In recognition of the *special educational needs* of children of *low-income families* and the impact that concentrations of low-income families have on the ability of local educational agencies to support adequate educational programs, the Congress hereby declares it to be the policy

27

of the United States to provide financial assistance to local educational agencies serving areas with concentrations of children from low-income families to expand and improve their educational programs by various means which contribute particularly to meeting the special educational needs of educationally deprived children.[2] (emphasis added)

This statement of policy forms the basis for a series of provisions that local districts must satisfy to receive grants under Title I. First, the class of intended beneficiaries is specified—educationally deprived children residing in low-income areas (funds allocation provisions). Second, the requirements attempt to maximize the likelihood that Title I funds will be used effectively to meet the needs of such children in two ways: by requiring that funds be allocated only for programs intended to expand and improve the regular program (supplemental provisions), and that programs be properly designed and implemented (program development provisions). Third, a means is provided for verifying fund and program accountability (accountability provision). Finally, the relationship between federal and state and local compensatory educational funds is explicated (coordination provisions).

In this chapter we describe the federal legal framework which governed the use of Title I funds by local school districts prior to the Education Amendments of 1978. This framework consists of the statutory provisions enacted by Congress, as well as the legislative and interpretive rules developed by the federal government to ensure that states and school districts understand and comply with the purpose of the program. Legislative rules are defined as "rules . . . issued by an agency pursuant to statutory authority which implement the statute."[3] Such rules have the "full force and effect of law." For Title I they include the regulations and mandatory criteria contained in guidelines developed by the U.S. Office of Education, the federal agency responsible for administering the law. An interpretive rule is defined as "a rule or statement issued by an agency to advise the public of the agency's practical interpretation of the statutes and rules that it administers."[4] In the case of Title I, the interpretive rules are contained in such documents as handbooks and correspondence between OE and individual states. These rules are intended to bring about distributive equity with respect to Title I resources; that is, they govern which children receive what kinds of Title I services.[5]

FUNDS ALLOCATION PROVISIONS

Congress recognized that federal appropriations of Title I funds would generally not be sufficient to serve all educationally deprived children in a school district. To prevent dilution of Title I funds, Congress decided to concentrate these limited resources in areas determined to be in greatest need of assistance, namely, areas having high concentrations of children from low-income families. To this end, the regulations and guidelines issued by OE contain eligibility and targeting requirements.

In brief, school districts are required to make a series of decisions in allocating Title I funds to various schools and children within their boundaries. Districts must:

> determine eligible school attendance areas on the basis of concentration of children from low-income families;[6]
>
> select target areas, that is, decide which of the eligible attendance areas will receive Title I services[7] (generally, districts must select those areas with the highest incidence of low-income families and, within those areas, the educationally deprived children who are "most in need of assistance");[8]
>
> distribute funds to targeted areas;
>
> determine eligible children in target schools on the basis of educational criteria; and
>
> select target children, that is, decide which of the eligible children will receive Title I services.

In reality, the decision-making process is not as orderly as the process suggested here. Rather than follow a sequence of steps, school districts make decisions simultaneously in many cases.

School Eligibility Requirements[9]

According to the Title I legislation, not all areas within a school district are eligible to receive assistance under Title I. The legislation provides that Title I funds may be used by school districts for programs and projects " which are designed to meet the special educational needs of educationally deprived children in school attendance areas having high concentrations of children from low-income families."[10] The regulations do not define a particular income level as "low-income" nor do they specify the means to be used in determining income level. The level suggested in an OE program guide issued in 1968 has long since become outdated.

The regulations do include certain prescriptions, however. First, the regulations specify that available data should be used to make "an accurate determination of the number of children from low-income families."[11] Second, where data are not available to make an accurate determination of the number of children, "the number may be estimated on the basis of the number of children in families receiving AFDC [Aid to Families with Dependent Children], the number of children eligible to receive benefits under the National School Lunch Act, or any other reliable and uniform indicator of poverty, or a combination of such factors."[12] According to the OE publication, *Title I ESEA: Selecting Target Areas,* such indicators might include school surveys, health, housing or employment statistics. Finally, the regulations provide that "whatever data are used must be applied uniformly throughout the applicant's school district."[13]

According to the regulations issued by OE, a district may use either of two methods to determine which school attendance areas within the district have "high concentrations of children from low-income families." According to the "percentage method," which is the more commonly used of the two methods, only those school attendance areas with a *percentage* of children from low-income families as high as the districtwide average are eligible to participate in Title I programs. According to the "numerical method," only those school attendance areas in which the *number* of such children is as large as the average number of such children per attendance area in the district are eligible.[14]

In addition, the regulations permit a district to rank some areas on one basis and some on the other. However, if a combination of methods is used, "the number of attendance areas actually designated ... may *not* exceed the number of such areas that could be so designated if only one such method had been used." [15] (emphasis added)

The potential effect of such local discretion is demonstrated by the analysis of the hypothetical (but not improbable) district described in Figure 2-1. Attendance area 1 has the highest number of children from low-income families; however, it also has a disproportionately high total number of students, so that its low-income children constitute a small percentage (16.67 percent) of the school population. By the percentage method, attendance area 1 fails to qualify for Title I funds, since the percentage of poor children in residence falls short of the districtwide average (22 percent). Attendance areas 2 and 3 qualify by this method.

If the numerical method is applied, the eligibility of the schools is exactly reversed: only attendance area 1 has a greater number of poor students (100) than the average for the district (67); attendance areas 2 and 3 do not qualify.

Again, districts also have the option of using both the percentage and numerical methods, ranking some areas on one basis and some

FIGURE 2-1. GENERAL ELIGIBILITY RULES APPLIED TO THREE ATTENDANCE AREAS WITHIN A HYPOTHETICAL DISTRICT

NUMBER/PERCENTAGE OF CHILDREN	DISTRICT	AREA 1	AREA 2	AREA 3	AREA AVERAGE
Total number	1,000	600	200	200	333
Number from low-income families	200	100	50	50	67
Percentage from low-income families	20%	16.67%	25%	25%	22%
Eligibility by numerical method		Eligible	Not eligible	Not eligible	
Eligibility by percentage method		Not eligible	Eligible	Eligible	

on the other. The only restriction in using such a procedure is that the number of attendance areas actually designated as eligible may not exceed the number of such areas that could be so designated if only one method were used. In our hypothetical district the percentage method would yield two eligible attendance areas, so only two of the three attendance areas can be deemed eligible using the combined percentage and numerical ranking. In view of the flexibility of the Title I legal framework, it would appear that this hypothetical district may choose the two areas as it wishes.

In addition to these general rules for determining eligibility, there are other ways in which areas can qualify for Title I. These exceptions in the law and regulations include the *no wide variance* provision, the *formerly eligible* provision, the *enrollment* option, and the *30 percent* option.

The *no wide variance* provision reflects the fact that if all school attendance areas have approximately the same incidence of poverty, the poverty criterion will be of little value in determining eligibility. Thus, the regulations provide that "if there is no wide variance in the concentrations of children from low-income families among the several school attendance areas in a school district, the whole of that school district may at the option of the [district] be regarded as a project area."[16] The regulations contain an objective criterion for determining when no wide variance exists. The district may make such a determination " only if the variation between the areas with the highest and the lowest percentage of such children is not more than one-third of the average percentage of children from low-income families in the district as a whole."[17]

In order to provide a degree of continuity, the *formerly eligible* provision prevents a school from losing its eligibility because of a change in its ranking. Prior to 1974 a school attendance area which was designated as a project area for a particular year could not continue to be designated as a project area during the next year if it failed to meet the general eligibility requirements described above. The Education Amendments of 1974 provide that an eligible attendance area which has been selected as a project area may continue to be eligible for at least two additional years.[18]

The third exception is commonly called the *enrollment* option. It permits the district, under certain conditions, to provide Title I services to certain public schools in ineligible school attendance areas. The Education Amendments of 1974 state that a district may, "at its discretion," use Title I funds for educationally deprived children attending a school not located in an eligible school attendance area if "the proportion of children in actual average daily attendance from low-income families is substantially the same as the proportion of such children" in an eligible attendance area.[19]

The regulations provide a standard to determine when this enrollment option may be used by a district. Title I services may be provided to a public school in an ineligible school attendance area "if the percentage or number of children from low-income families in average daily attendance at that school is at least as high as the districtwide average percentage or number required" for eligibility on the basis of attendance in accordance with the general rules described above.[20]

The last exception is the *30 percent* option. As already explained, a school attendance area may be considered eligible for participation in a Title I program if the percentage of children from low-income families in that area is at least as high as the percentage of such children districtwide (the percentage method). In addition, a district may specifically request that attendance areas in which at least 30 percent of the children are from low-income families be approved for participation in Title I, even where the districtwide average is substantially higher.[21]

Each of these exceptions may be of special importance in achieving equity in school districts undergoing desegregation. The no wide variance and 30 percent exceptions recognize the fact that desegregation plans may disperse children from low-income families more evenly throughout the district. In the former case, the district may elect to declare all schools eligible, if they can meet the required standard; in the latter case, it may decide to serve schools which have the required minimum concentration of low-income students. Where school attendance areas remain unchanged, the formerly eligible option takes into account the potential disruption in services which may be brought about by the sudden shift in school attendance patterns accompanying school desegregation. The enrollment option may be useful in districts where school attendance no longer reflects neighborhood boundaries.

School Targeting Requirements

Having developed a list of eligible attendance areas, the district must choose which schools it will "target," that is, fund. The law and regulations impose two related constraints on district choice. The first is the legislative requirement that payments under Title I must be used for programs and projects "which are of sufficient size, scope, and quality to give reasonable promise of substantial progress" toward meeting the needs of educationally deprived children in low-income areas.[22] The regulations explain that this *concentration* provision may be satisfied by limiting either the number of children or the number of areas.

The concentration requirement, which is intended to increase program quality, is based on a simple premise: if funds are spread so thinly that children receive few extra services or only brief exposure to the services provided, little or no progress will be made. Decisions to limit the number of participants to ensure program effectiveness—so that the services provided are likely to increase substantially the educational attainment of the children served—are difficult and sometimes painful to make. If the concentration requirement did not exist, district officials might succumb to pressures to serve everyone or implement numerous "pet projects."

The regulations do not provide specific standards for meeting the concentration requirement. The absence of standards appears to reflect OE's position that it is the responsibility of the state educational agency to take the initiative in promulgating standards to ensure sufficient concentration of Title I services.

Two types of guidelines were employed by OE in the past to guide district compliance with the concentration requirement. The first concerned dollar allocation: the total amount of dollars spent on each Title I project participant should equal roughly half the level of state and local expenditures per student. The second type of guideline concerned the educational effectiveness of each activity within a Title I project. It consisted of quantitative indicators, such as student-teacher ratio for the activity, frequency with which the activity was pursued, duration of the activity, and number of activity periods scheduled for the project.[23]

The second and closely related constraint on targeting is the *no-skip* provision, which governs the designation of project areas from among those eligible.[24] This provision states that a district may not designate a school attendance area as a project area "unless all attendance areas with a higher percentage or number of children of low-income families . . . have been so designated." However, if the district can argue successfully to its state educational agency that it can serve all eligible attendance areas with sufficient concentration to meet the vague legal standard, the no-skip regulation is waived.

It is important to point out that the number of children to be served will also be a key determinant in school targeting. Assume that an initial decision has been made on the number of students to be served at three eligible schools, as illustrated in Figure 2-2. Though all three attendance areas are eligible for Title I funding, serving all 600 students identified in the three eligible schools will probably result in a level of funding per student which is unacceptably low.

The law and regulations offer the district confronted with this situation two alternatives. It can follow the no-skip regulation, that is, not target the lowest ranked or the two lowest ranked schools, thereby achieving an acceptably high level of concentration per student in the remaining school(s) to be served. Or it can target fewer students at each school and serve all schools. In either case, the expenditure per student is increased. Decisions on school and student targeting are probably made simultaneously at the district level because of the intimate relationship between the decisions made in fulfilling the concentration requirement.

There are three exceptions to the no-skip rule. First, a district may skip a higher ranked school if a lower ranked school has a "substantially" higher incidence of educational deprivation. Specifically, the regulations provide that a higher ranked school may be skipped "if such agency can demonstrate, to the satisfaction of the State educational agency, that the incidence and severity of educational deprivation in [the area having a higher incidence of low-income families] is substantially less than in other attendance areas proposed to be designated."[25]

Under these circumstances the regulations provide that a skipped school may *not* be included in the nonproject area average for purposes of computing comparability, and the district must in fact demonstrate that the skipped school is comparable to the nonproject area school average.[26] If a state educational agency does not first make this required determination, then it cannot approve the district's request for an exception.

The "formerly eligible" exception to the general eligibility rules also serves as an exception to the targeting requirements. Thus, a school previously designated as a project area school may continue to be so designated for an additional two years, even if it is no longer one of the highest ranked schools.

Finally, a district may skip a higher ranked school attendance area if it has been designated "to receive [through the use of funds

FIGURE 2-2. GENERAL TARGETING RULES APPLIED TO THREE ATTENDANCE AREAS WITHIN A HYPOTHETICAL DISTRICT*

TARGETING DECISION	AVAILABLE DISTRICT FUNDING	STUDENTS TARGETED IN AREA 1 (HIGHEST RANKING)	STUDENTS TARGETED: AREA 2	STUDENTS TARGETED: AREA 3	DOLLARS PER STUDENT
Serve all students selected in all eligible schools	$600,000	300	200	100	$100
Follow the no-skip regulation	60,000	300	None	None	200
Serve fewer students in all eligible schools	60,000	150	100	500	200

*Based on the assumption that Areas 1, 2, and 3 have been identified as eligible, with a total of 600 students eligible to be served by Title I.

from other sources] services of the same nature and scope as those that would otherwise be provided under Title I"—for example, state compensatory educational funds.[27]

Distributing Funds to Targeted Areas

Once the eligibility of schools has been determined and specific schools have been targeted to receive Title I services, districts have discretion in distributing resources to the targeted schools. There is no express requirement that participating schools in areas with higher concentrations of children from low-income families receive funds in proportion to the needs of the educationally deprived children in those areas. The only written policy concerning proportional distribution was contained in *Program Guide No. 44,* which was issued in 1968 and has since been cancelled. Section 4.6 generally provided that Title I programs must be conducted in a limited number of eligible areas and must provide relatively higher concentrations of services in areas having the highest incidence of poverty.[28]

As might be expected, there is considerable variance in the interpretation and implementation of the requirements governing the distribution of funds to targeted areas. Districts operate with various explicit and/or inferred instructions.

If we return to the example in Figure 2-1, using the percentage criterion to determine school eligibility, attendance areas 2 and 3 are both eligible; each has 500 students whose families are poor. The district may decide that the needs of the students in each school are the same and that the same proportion of students in each school is needy. (Need is based on educational disadvantage without regard to poverty.) The district would then allocate approximately 50 percent of available resources to each school. However, the district might decide that the need is greater in area 2 than in area 3. This could be determined on the basis of the proportion of students with educational disadvantage, on the basis of the degree or intensity of disadvantage (for example, how far below average test scores fall), or on the basis of the type of educational disadvantage (for example, low test scores on reading versus low test scores on math). The result could be that, given two schools with the same number of poor students, the same proportion of poor students, and even possibly the same proportion of educationally disadvantaged students, one school is allocated considerably more resources than the other.

Student Eligibility and Targeting Requirements

The purpose of Title I, as set forth in the legislation, is to provide financial assistance to school districts so that they can meet the special educational needs of educationally deprived children who reside in low-income areas. Therefore, the regulations provide that after project areas have been chosen, *educational deprivation* rather than *economic deprivation* is the sole criterion for determining which students are eligible to participate in Title I programs and for selecting from among the eligible students those who will actually participate in the programs. With respect to selecting which children will participate, the districts must generally select those who are "most in need" of assistance. In other words, there are three criteria (subject to certain exceptions described below) a student must meet to be selected for participation in a Title I program. The student must (1) reside in a project area; (2) be educationally deprived, regardless of family income; and (3) be most in need of assistance. The first criterion has already been fully described.

With respect to the second criterion, the Title I statute does not define the term "educationally deprived children." However, it is defined in the Title I regulations as "(1) children who have need for special educational assistance in order that their level of educational attainment may be raised to that appropriate for children of their age, and (2) children who are handicapped."[29]

Three important points contained in this definition require special emphasis. First, since the "appropriate" level of educational attainment is not spelled out, districts are given a great deal of flexibility in defining educational disadvantage. Second, as we observed above, although school attendance areas are selected on the basis of economic criteria, children residing in project areas are selected on the basis of educational deprivation, irrespective of the income of their parents or other noneducational considerations. Thus, students who are poor or who are culturally, racially, or linguistically isolated from the community at large but who do not satisfy the educational criteria set forth above are not eligible for assistance under Title I.[30] The reverse is also true: the regulations provide that "a child may not be excluded from participating in a project because he or she is not from a low-income family."[31] Finally, handicapped children are considered educationally deprived for purposes of Title I. The third criterion concerns the targeting of program participants.

Since Title I has never been fully funded by Congress, it is generally the case that a district will be unable to serve all educationally deprived students residing in low-income areas. Therefore, the district must select from among the eligible students those who will actually participate in the Title I program. The decision involves two steps. First, based on a review of "existing data ... on the performance in the agency's basic programs of instruction of [eligible] children," a district must select the "age or grade levels at which it will operate the Title I project [or projects]."[32] For example, the district may choose to serve only those students in kindergarten through grade six. It may choose to serve handicapped children or it may choose not to.[33] Second, the district must select the students within these groups who will participate in the Title I program. Again, those selected must be the educationally deprived students in each group who are most in need of special assistance.[34]

The regulations specify that a district may, at its discretion, target students who are *not* "most in need" of assistance if three criteria are met.[35] Such students must (1) reside in the project area; (2) have participated in a project conducted in the previous year (that is, they were identified as being most in need during the previous year); and (3) still be educationally deprived (that is, they are still performing below the level appropriate for their age). The purpose of this provision is to enable school districts to build upon progress made in previous years.

A second exception involves participation by students from outside the project area. According to the general school attendance area rules, only educationally deprived students residing in project areas may participate in Title I programs. However, under certain circumstances, the regulations authorize participation by eligible students who do *not* reside in the project area. Four criteria must be met before such students may participate: (1) they must meet all participation criteria other than residency, (2) their participation must not result in the exclusion of children from the project area who meet participation criteria, (3) the project must be designed for the children selected from the project area, and (4) such participation must neither impair the effectiveness of the project nor result in any extra cost.[36] These criteria serve to protect against the diminution of services to students in eligible attendance areas.

SUPPLEMENTAL PROVISIONS

Six additional requirements are designed to ensure that Title I funds are used only to "expand and improve" programs for educationally deprived students residing in low-income areas. In order to ensure that Title I funds meet the students' "special" (as opposed to regular or ordinary) needs, discrimination with respect to the distribution of state and local funds is prohibited, and a certain minimum level of state and local support must be provided. The requirements vary according to whether they apply at the district, school, or student level, and whether they refer to funds or services.

General aid provisions require that Title I programs contribute to meeting the special educational needs of the intended beneficiaries. These provisions prohibit the use of Title I funds to meet the general needs of the student body at large, however pressing those needs may be.[37]

Maintenance-of-effort provisions apply to district-level expenditures and require that funding from state and local sources not decrease.[38] Without such provisions, states or districts could substitute Title I dollars for their own money and maintain the same level of overall educational expenditures. This requirement is designed to ensure that federal assistance serves a supplemental rather than a basic educational function and to prevent Title I grantees from shifting their financial responsibility for basic educational programs to the federal government.

Comparability provisions apply at the school level to the services provided from state and local funds. Generally, they require that the level of these services in every Title I school be comparable, that is, roughly equal to the average level in non-Title I schools before the addition of Title I funds.[39] These provisions are designed to ensure that federal assistance is not used to support a level of services that is already available in non-Title I schools in the district. Comparability is generally measured in terms of two factors: the ratio of pupil to staff and per pupil expenditures.

Supplement-not-supplant provisions apply to the use of funds at the student level.[40] Intended to ensure that Title I funds add to rather than replace state and local funds, they add significantly to the restrictions on local spending behavior contained in the maintenance-of-effort and comparability requirements. Children in Title I programs must receive the same level of state and local funds they would have received if Title I did not exist. They cannot be penalized in the provision of state and local funds because they receive assistance under Title I.

The *excess cost* requirement clarifies the supplement-not-supplant provisions by stipulating that Title I funds can pay only for the excess costs of Title I programs and projects.[41] If, for example, a district is spending an average of $1,000 per pupil for the regular academic program, and the local Title I program is designed to provide a more intensive version of the same program, Title I may pay only for the costs of the program that are in excess of $1,000 per pupil. In 1974 Congress clarified the meaning of excess costs by explaining that, in computing the state and local base, the district may exclude, among other things, expenditures for state and local compensatory education programs similar to Title I.[42]

The supplement-not-supplant and excess cost requirements are closely related. The first prevents districts from penalizing students in Title I programs when allocating state and local funds. The second ensures that Title I funds pay only the costs of services beyond normal instructional expenditures.

The *equitably provided* requirement, formerly termed "ordinarily provided," extends the comparability regulations from the school to the student level and uses a different measure of services.[43] Comparability of services offered by Title I and non-Title I schools is determined by such broad tests as the ratio of pupil to staff. The equitably provided requirement ensures that Title I students in Title I schools, as a group, receive their fair share of specific services in comparison to children in non-Title I schools. This requirement applies when districts are introducing a new, locally provided service to some but not all children. For example, if a district implements a new compensatory reading program, the equitably provided rule requires that the proportion of Title I students involved in the new program be comparable to their proportion among all students in the district.

As a whole, the rules governing funds allocation and the supplemental provisions give force to the statutory intent that Title I funds be used to "expand and improve" programs by meeting the "special" needs of educationally deprived children in low-income areas.

PROGRAM DEVELOPMENT REQUIREMENTS

Program development requirements establish the procedures that districts must follow in designing and implementing Title I programs. Six major requirements are designed to ensure that the services provided are related to the needs of the children to be served and that they are carefully planned, implemented, and evaluated.

The first program development requirement governs the *nature of the program*. The Title I legal framework requires that funds be used to meet the special educational needs of educationally deprived children residing in low-income areas. The focus of programs must be educational, although the legal framework clearly permits the use of Title I funds to pay for "auxiliary services." For example, health or welfare services, which are unavailable under other programs and which support an educational objective can be funded under Title I; however, Title I cannot be recast as a health or welfare program.[44]

The *needs assessment* requirement is the first step in the program development process and involves identifying educationally disadvantaged children and specifying their needs.[45] It serves several purposes. Without a comprehensive assessment of children's needs, certain children residing in low-income areas who are in need of special assistance might be missed, whereas parents of other children having less need for special assistance might successfully lobby for inclusion of their children in the Title I program. Needs assessment enables districts to resist such pressures. Also, in the absence of such a requirement, districts could use Title I funds to meet low-priority needs rather than those which are most pressing. Finally, a needs assessment increases the likelihood that the educational strategies chosen will be related to the specific needs of the children to be served.

The *program design* requirement calls for a formal plan establishing objectives for the Title I program, based on the results of the needs assessment, and specifying activities to accomplish these ends.[46] Identification of program objectives provides a clear direction for program activities. In addition, objectives become the criteria against which success can be measured. Strategies must be formulated purposefully so that Title I programs are planned rather than determined merely by custom or inertia, and so that district staff use their best judgment to develop program activities that will accomplish objectives. The program design requirements thus provide a link between needs assessment and program implementation.

The *coordination* requirement is included in the Title I legal framework to avoid duplication of benefits and to ensure the most efficient use of Title I funds in meeting the special educational needs of program participants.[47] Districts must first use whatever assistance is available from other sources before using Title I funds for auxiliary services.

The *program evaluation* requirement ensures that the effects of Title I programs are assessed and that the results of these assessments are used by the districts to determine how their programs might be improved.[48] Evaluation results must also be reported to state educational agencies.

The *parent involvement* requirement is based on two premises.[49] First, when parents are involved in the planning, implementation, and evaluation of programs for their children, there is a greater interest on the part of both parents and children in making the program successful.[50] Second, there is a greater likelihood that Title I funds will be used for well-planned programs for the intended beneficiaries if the parents of the beneficiaries are authorized to oversee program implementation. The Title I statute and regulations generally provide that a district establish a districtwide parent advisory council and an advisory council at each project area school. Parent advisory councils must be involved in the planning, implementation, and evaluation of local Title I programs.

ACCOUNTABILITY PROVISIONS

The final category of requirements, which includes the *reporting,*[51] *record-keeping,*[52] and *access to information*[53] provisions, is designed to ensure fund and program accountability. These requirements provide a means for verifying compliance with the other Title I legal requirements described above (for example, the requirement that Title I funds be used only to meet the needs of educationally deprived children residing in low-income areas and that they supplement, not supplant, state and local funds).

COORDINATING TITLE I AND STATE OR LOCAL COMPENSATORY EDUCATION PROGRAMS

In the past several years many states and local school districts have enacted compensatory education programs.[54] The Title I legal framework permits districts to coordinate the distribution of Title I and other compensatory funds and jointly plan programs receiving assistance from both sources as long as certain rules are satisfied.[55] The first rule is that, as a group, educationally deprived students residing in areas with large concentrations of students from low-income families (that is, areas eligible for assistance under Title I), must receive their fair share of compensatory funds.[56] Fair share is determined in accordance with an objective criterion established under state or local law for distributing such funds. For example, if state law provides that compensatory funds must be used for students scoring below the 25th percentile on a standardized achievement test and 75 percent of these students reside in Title I-eligible areas, then 75 percent of the compensatory funds must be spent in Title I-eligible areas.

The standards for designing and implementing coordinated programs are contained in a second rule, which states that a district may use Title I and other compensatory funds *simultaneously,* provided it can demonstrate that Title I funds are used for students and components of projects meeting all the Title I requirements.[57] OE has described several approaches to comprehensive planning, each reflecting a different way of varying two factors: children served and services provided.[58]

Title I and other funds can be used to pay for *different services* to the *same students.* For example, the district may decide to fund the remedial reading program within Title I project areas with Title I funds, and use other compensatory funds for the remedial math program. Or the school district might use Title I funds to pay for all instructional salaries and use other compensatory funds to pay for materials, supplies, and equipment.

Alternatively, compensatory education funds can be used to provide the *same services* to *different students.* For example, a district might use state and local funds to serve students in kindergarten through grade six and use Title I funds for grades seven through twelve. Or a district might use nonfederal funds for a certain group of students within a particular grade span and use Title I funds for the other students within that grade span.

A third approach is to distribute state or local compensatory funds to schools according to the relative number or percentage of educationally deprived students enrolled in each school (ranking schools). Educationally deprived children attending schools which receive these monies and which also qualify for assistance under Title I can be skipped if they are offered services of the same nature and scope as would have been provided under Title I. Title I funds can then be used in other eligible schools.

CONCLUSION

Thus, the rules governing local behavior are primarily designed to limit the use of Title I funds for intended beneficiaries and purposes and to ensure that the services offered are carefully designed and implemented to meet the special needs of recipients. Although the rules are extremely detailed and complicated, they also allow for considerable flexibility. Some rules are subject to broad interpretation; others allow various options and exceptions; still others suggest standards but do not require them. School districts that understand their legal options can exercise considerable discretion within the Title I legal framework. However, as we shall see in the following chapter, the complexity of the rules often invites varying interpretations, some of which are unnecessarily restrictive. Thus, local behavior is very much a function of how the rules are interpreted and enforced.

Notes

1. The term "state educational agency" refers to "the officer or agency primarily responsible for the state supervision of public elementary and secondary schools." Section 403(7) of P.L. 81-874.

2. Section 101 of Title I (20 U.S.C. 241a).

3. Kenneth Davis, *Administrative Law Text* (St. Paul, Minn.: West Publishing, 1972), p. 126.

4. NIE, *Administration of Compensatory Education* (Washington, D.C.: NIE, September 19, 1977), pp. 5-6.

5. Distributive equity is also a function of the different funds allocated to local school districts. These amounts depend on (1) the overall amount of funding appropriated by Congress, (2) county-level entitlements based on a standard formula, and (3) subcounty allocation procedures which vary by state. For a complete discussion of these procedures and their impact on distributive equity at the school district level, see NIE, *Title I Funds Allocation: The Current Formula* (Washington, D.C.: NIE, September 30, 1977).

6. 45 C.F.R. 116a.20 (1976) and 45 C.F.R. 116a.21(c) (1976). The term "school attendance area" means "in relation to a particular public school, the geographical area in which the children who are normally served by that school reside." 45 C.F.R. 116a.2 (1976).

7. 45 C.F.R. 116a.20(c) (1976) and 45 C.F.R. 116a.21(e) (1976).

8. The eligibility and targeting requirements ensure that districts do not discriminate against children qualifying for Title I services simply because those children attend private schools.

9. It should be pointed out that the regulations include a provision which expressly authorizes application of the school attendance area eligibility and targeting requirements separately by grade span. They also specify that the grade span groupings used for purposes of making school attendance area eligibility and targeting decisions must be the same groups used by the district for purposes of reporting comparability. 45 C.F.R. 116a.20(b)(5) (1976).

10. Section 141(a)(1)(A) of Title 1 [20 U.S.C. 241e(a)(1)(A)].

11. 45 C.F.R. 116a.20(f) (1976).

12. Ibid.

13. Ibid.

14. 45 C.F.R. 116a.20(b)(2) and (3) (1976).

15. 45 C.F.R. 116a.20(b)(4) (1976).

16. 45.C.F.R. 116a.20(d) (1976).

17. Ibid. However, since the concentration requirement [45 C.F.R. 116a.22(b) (5) (1976)] must still be met, this does not necessarily mean that all the schools within a district may be targeted as project areas. See below for a description of the targeting requirements.

18. 45 C.F.R. 116a.20(g) (1976).

19. Section 141(a)(1)(A) of Title I [20 U.S.C. 241e(a)(1)(A)]. The legislative history accompanying the 1974 Education Amendments explains the purpose of this exception. "Existing law links eligibility as a Title I school with the location of the school in an attendance area with a high concentration of children from low-income families. However, in some school districts, because of the attendance of children in nonpublic schools, the economic composition of the attendance area served by a public school is not reflective of the economic level of the children actually enrolled. Existing law would bar the designation of such a school, even though its actual enrollment would qualify it to be a Title I target school under the poverty criteria utilized by the school district." Senate Report No. 93-763, 93d Congress, 2d Session 30 (1974).

20. 45 C.F.R. 116a.20(h) (1976). The enrollment option presumes that the district has completed the ranking of attendance areas based on either the percentage or number of low-income children residing in the attendance area.

21. 45 C.F.R. 116a.20 (b) (2) (1976). For purposes of the 30 percent option only children who are determined to be eligible for free lunches, pursuant to criteria established by the state educational agency in accordance with the National School Lunch Act (42 U.S.C. 1758b) and regulations (7 C.F.R. 245), may be counted.

22. Section 141(a)(1)(B) of Title I [20 U.S.C. 241e(a)(1)(B)].

23. See HEW, *ESEA Title I Program Guide No. 44* (Washington, D.C.: Office of Education, 1968), Sections 4.7 and 5.1.

24. 45 C.F.R. 116a.20(c)(1) (1976). The term "project area" means "an attendance area, or combination of attendance areas, having a high concentration of children from low-income families which, without regard to the locality of the project itself, is designated as an area from which children are to be selected to participate in a project." 45 C.F.R. 116a.2 (1976).

25. 45 C.F.R. 116a.20(c)(2) (1976).

26. Ibid.

27. 45 C.F.R. 116a.20(c)(1) (1976).

28. Section 4.6 of *Program Guide No. 44* states: "The applicant should make sure that the needs of children in eligible areas with the highest incidence of poverty have been met before considering the needs of children in eligible areas in which the incidence is much lower. The program in the areas with the highest incidence should be designed to serve a larger proportion of children and to provide them with a greater variety of services than programs in areas with lesser incidences of poverty."

29. 45 C.F.R. 116a.2 (1979). The question has been raised whether Title I funds may be used to meet the needs of "underachievers." OE has responded as follows: "The term 'underachiever' is used to describe children whose performance is considered not to be commensurate with their potential.... The children in Title I programs in general tend to be 'underachievers' *but* the starting point for a Title I program is the identification of the children who are 'below grade level'...."

30. The definition of the term "educationally deprived children" set forth in the *old* regulations [45 C.F.R. 116.1(i) (1974)] included a statement specifying possible causal factors for a child's educational deprivation, such as "poverty, neglect, delinquency, or cultural or linguistic isolation from the community at large." The inclusion of these causal factors was misconstrued by some persons to mean that if a child was linguistically isolated or poor, he or she would be deemed eligible, irrespective of the child's level of educational attainment. The revised regulations, as quoted in the text, have deleted this statement of causal factors.

31. 45 C.F.R. 116a.21(e) (1976).

32. 45 C.F.R. 116a.21(a) (1976).

33. 45 C.F.R. 116a.21(b) (1976). Districts must comply with 45 C.F.R. 116.40 (b) (1976), entitled "Services which applicant is required to provide." This subsection prohibits the use of Title I funds for services which a district is required to provide (1) by state law; (2) pursuant to a formal determination under Title VI of the Civil Rights Act, Title IX of the Educational Amendments of 1972 (P.L. 92-318), or Section 504 of the Rehabilitation Act of 1973, as amended; or (3) pursuant to a final order of a court. Handicapped children may still be served under Title I, but any use of Title I funds for this purpose is subject to 45 C.F.R. 116.40(b).

34. 45 C.F.R. 116a.21(d) (1976).

35. 45 C.F.R. 116a.21(e) (1976). The comments preceding the regulations explain that this exception to "the greatest need" targeting standard was added to give districts the discretion to serve such children. See Comment 5 on 116a.21,

41 FR 42898 (September 28, 1976). That OE did not intend to distinguish between children "most in need" and those with "the greatest need" can be inferred from the synonymous usage of these terms in the regulations. Compare 45 C.F.R. 116a.21(d) (1976) with 45 C.F.R. 116a.21(e) (1976).

36. 45 C.F.R. 116a.22(b)(9) (i) (ii) (iii) (iv) (1976). The comments preceding the regulation state that even if these criteria are met, the district "has the discretion to not serve such children." See comment on 116a.19, 41 FR 42397-42898 (September 28, 1976).

37. Section 101 of Title I (20 U.S.C. 241a); 45 C.F.R. 116a.22 (b) (4) (iii), (b) (6), (b) (7) and (b) (8) (1976).

38. Section 143 (c) (2) of Title I [20 U.S.C. 241g (c) (2)] ; 45 C.F.R. 116.19 (1976).

39. Section 141 (a) (3) (C) [20 U.S.C. 241e (a) (3)(C)] ; 45 C.F.R. 116a.26 (1976).

40. Section 141(a) (3) (B) of Title I [20 U.S.C. 241(e) (a) (3) (B)] ; 45 C.F.R. 116.40 (1976). Prior to 1976 these provisions applied also at the school level.

41. Section 141(a) (1) of Title I [20 U.S.C. 241e (a) (1)] ; 45 C.F.R. 116.40 (a) (2) (iii) (1976).

42. The Title I regulations include four criteria for determining whether a state compensatory education program qualifies for the exemption. First, the funds must be used for educationally deprived children. Second, the funds must be used for a program that is evaluated. Third, funds must be used for special, supplementary purposes. Fourth, the district must be accountable to the state educational agency for compliance with the first three requirements.

43. 45 C.F.R. 116a.22 (b) (19) (1976).

44. See 45 C.F.R. 116.41 (1976).

45. 45 C.F.R. 116a.21 (1976).

46. 45 C.F.R. 116a.22 (a) (1) (1976), 116a.22 (b) (1) (1976), 116a.19 (b), and 116a.22 (1976).

47. 45 C.F.R. 116.41 (1976).

48. Section 141(a) (6) and 141(a) (7) of Title I [20 U.S.C. 241e (a) (6) and (a) (7)] ; 45 C.F.R. 116.43 (1976).

49. Section 141(a) (14) of Title I [20 U.S.C. 241e (a) (14)] ; 45 C.F.R. 116a.25 (1976).

50. This legislative premise described in the text is expressly set forth in the legislative history. House Report No. 93-805, 3 *U.S. Code, Congressional and Administrative News* 4109 (1974).

51. Section 141(a) (7) of Title I [20 U.S.C. 241e (a) (7)] ; 45 C.F.R. 116.46 (1976).

52. Section 141(a) (7) and (a) (8) of Title I [20 U.S.C. 241e (a) (7) and (a) (8); 45 C.F.R. 116.45 (1976).

53. Ibid.

54. See NIE, *Administration of Compensatory Education,* chapter 5; and NIE, *State Compensatory Education Programs* (Washington, D.C.: NIE, 1978).

55. See Robert Silverstein et al., *A Description and Analysis of the Relationship Between Title I, ESEA and Selected State Compensatory Education Programs* (Washington, D.C.: Lawyers' Committee for Civil Rights Under Law, September 1977).

56. Ibid., chapter 8.

57. 45 C.F.R. 116.41 (1976).

58. See Silverstein et al., *Description and Analysis,* chapter 10.

3

Administration
of Title I

The legal framework of Title I is intended to direct the behavior of
local school districts in determining which schools and students receive what special services as a consequence of Title I funding. Yet
the rules do not fully determine the ways in which school districts
allocate and utilize these funds. Variation in local behavior is partly
by design; the rules permit a great deal of flexibility in local implementation of federal policy. Variation is also a function of the manner
in which the rules are written and communicated, and the degree to
which compliance is monitored and enforced. That is, local behavior
is also dependent on the way in which the Title I program is administered. In this chapter we focus on the administration of Title I—the
essential link between congressional intent and program implementation.

Over the years the administration of Title I has been the subject
of various criticisms.[1] Early critics directed their attention to two
types of problems. Some asserted that OE, the federal agency charged
with overall administration of the program, had too limited an administrative capacity to perform the essential management functions

51

necessary to guarantee faithful implementation of legislative intent.[2] Others argued that even with additional staff and other resources, implementation of Title I would be difficult to achieve. The intergovernmental linkages required to effect change were simply not sufficient to overcome state and local resistance to federal intervention.

Bailey and Mosher were among the first to call attention to the intergovernmental problems associated with implementing Title I within a complex, multilayered delivery system. While each layer in the system was given a set of roles and responsibilities, each also faced a unique set of limitations which severely restricted its ability to effect change.

> Title I established a pattern of intergovernmental relations which gave influence and responsibility to every level—local, state and federal. But it also set limits on that influence. The USOE by-passed the States in determining the initial allocation of grants. State officials had inherent supervisory power over the performance of local officials, but they were constrained in this case by criteria established at the Federal level. Local districts were given access to earmarked funds and latitude in designing programs to meet local conditions, but they remained circumscribed by State supervision.[3]

Kirst also identified fundamental structural problems in the intergovernmental chain:

> As in state government, we confront the problems of incentives and goal congruence—local goals may have a very different emphasis than the federal category. A federal goal of innovative programs for the disadvantaged may conflict with a local goal to provide a teacher salary increase and thereby stabilize property tax rates. In such cases, the administrative "muscle" of federal and state governments may not be sufficient to overcome local resistance or modification to better meet the local priority.[4]

Later studies by Berman and McLaughlin and by Rosenblum and Louis confirmed and extended early criticisms.[5] These authors helped expose the complications inherent in the assumption that educational innovation operates within a simple system in which change in one part of the system results in predictable impacts on the other parts.

As Rosenblum and Louis point out, a traditional systems approach presupposes the existence of strong linkages between the parts of the system. The educational system, however, is composed of multiple subsystems, which are only loosely linked or coupled with each other. Classrooms are bound together in schools; schools are parts of school districts; districts are grouped within state educational systems; and states are bound into the federal educational system. Because of longstanding traditions of local autonomy, the *formal* linkages between each of these subsystems become looser as one moves from the classroom upward. This loose coupling limits the degree to which changes initiated in one part of the system, such as those imposed from the top down, can result in the intended changes in other parts.

Arguing that change is not solely a rational process, these authors attacked the assumption that federal goals could be achieved simply by applying additional oversight and enforcement mechanisms. Federal efforts based on this assumption failed to recognize and build upon the *informal* linkages between subsystems—linkages based on shared professionalism and mutuality of goals and interests.

Recognition of informal linkages emerges when organizational change is viewed as a negotiated process, or a process involving mutual adaptation.[6] According to this theory, motivation for change, morale, goals, and competition within the system have as much, if not more, impact on implementation as either the initial stimulus for change or the formal enforcement mechanisms which accompany it.

Acceptance of this viewpoint militates against dependence on a management system which relies exclusively on formal means. In the case of Title I, it suggests capitalizing upon informal alliances among federal officials, Title I parents, and Title I program administrators. These relationships are presumed to exist within and across levels in the educational hierarchy. This view of the management process is perhaps best expressed by Hill:

> The management of Title I relies far more on techniques of informal political pressure, and less on formal methods of enforcement, than is generally recognized. Federal management is generally regarded as a process of enforcing specific provisions of law on local agencies through close monitoring of their performance and punishment of violators.... State and local policy is far more powerfully affected by subtler incentives implicit in federal officials' professional relationships with their counterparts at state and local levels, and on pressures for compliance generated by the press and by local beneficiary groups.[7]

In the following sections we describe the characteristics of the formal and informal management systems which govern Title I. Our major conclusion is that neither system could effectively function independently of the other. Each has a number of weaknesses; however, together the two systems complement one another in facilitating the implementation of federal policy.[8]

THE FORMAL MANAGEMENT SYSTEM

The formal Title I management system has evolved gradually since 1965. In the early years federal officials viewed Title I largely as a mechanism for distributing federal dollars. They were reluctant to perform more than a limited number of management functions: distributing funds, providing technical assistance to states and local school systems, and disseminating information. Proponents of this service delivery model of federal involvement argued that, since the constitution delegates responsibility for education to the states, federal intervention must be circumscribed.

The service delivery model appealed to federal administrators particularly during the early days of Title I. Born amid fears of a federal takeover in education and imposition of a national curriculum, Title I represented a compromise among various stakeholders in educational policy. State and local officials, together with other representatives of the educational establishment, were willing to give up a limited amount of local control in order to gain a great deal of federal money. In this sensitive political climate federal officials chose to distribute funds according to congressionally prescribed formulas without attaching too many strings.

Under this type of management, however, widespread misuse of funds occurred. Program expenditures violated legal requirements; many districts utilized the funds for general aid to all students, without regard to Title I eligibility.

In the late 1960s and early 1970s externally sponsored critiques, such as those by the NAACP Legal Defense and Education Fund and Jerome Murphy created pressures for improved program management.[9] As a result, the legal framework was revised and expanded to protect against certain types of abuses, and federal management practices were changed. The federal management system gradually shifted from a service to an enforcement model, based on the premise that when states and local districts accept federal funds they enter into a contractual agreement with the federal government. In order to ensure that the contract is fulfilled, the federal government has the right and responsibility to monitor state and local patterns of program delivery and expenditure and to apply sanctions where agencies are discovered to be out of compliance with federal requirements. In 1978 Hill argued that the formal management of Title I was founded entirely on an enforcement model.[10]

In reality, the service functions which must be performed in the management of Title I are closely related to enforcement mechanisms. Unlike federal programs such as Follow Through, Title I does not seek to bring about a particular educational innovation involving change in the philosophy, content, method, or organization of instruction. Title I is first and foremost a funds distribution (or redistribution) effort, in which large amounts of federal funds are earmarked for students in selected schools. In such a program, the role of the federal government differs from that of an external agent of change, such as a Follow Through sponsor. Instead of disseminating information on innovative curricula, teacher training techniques, or organizational change strategies, federal management focuses on interpreting the legal framework (rule making) and clarifying the federal rules sufficiently so that they guide, but do not unnecessarily constrain, local behavior. Federal technical assistance does not involve help in teacher training or curriculum development; it consists of responding to inquiries about federal rules and assisting state and local agencies to comply with federal requirements, including those governing the application and reporting process. Thus, the three components of the formal management system are rule making and dissemination, program monitoring, and enforcement of rules.

Rule Making and Dissemination

In its rule-making function, the federal government has constructed a legal framework which directs local school districts in the allocation and use of Title I funds, program design and implementation, and the relation of Title I funds to state and local expenditures. (These rules were described in detail in chapter two.) The framework also includes requirements for state administration and rules governing federal management.

It is almost impossible to separate the rule-making from the dissemination activities of OE. There are several vehicles for disseminating these rules. Regulations and formal guidelines are published in the *Federal Register* and distributed to all states and Title I districts. Interpretative statements are disseminated in written or oral form, typically in response to individual questions. Oral responses may be made via telephone, in national or regional workshops, or in the course of regular site visits.

Rule making and dissemination serve two important purposes. First, articulation of the legal framework is necessary to direct the behavior of local school systems in implementing federal policy with respect to Title I. Second, such articulation guides the behavior of state and federal officials who are charged with day-to-day oversight and overall management responsibility. Thus, it is important to examine rule making and dissemination to see how well they meet these ends.

The question of consistency in rule making is particularly significant given the history of changes in the legal framework. Congressional intent with respect to Title I policy has remained largely unchanged over time: Title I funds are to be used to produce real increases in district spending for education, not simply for tax relief. Furthermore, these increases are to be used for the delivery of additional services to specific children—educationally disadvantaged children in schools serving areas with high concentrations of poverty.

Nevertheless, the statutory provisions, legislative rules, and interpretive framework have been revised and extended a number of times. Generally these changes have been directed toward increased accountability, that is, ensuring that Title I funds are utilized in accordance with congressional intent. For example, as districts came to count on continued Title I funding, it became apparent that simply controlling Title I expenditures was not sufficient to ensure the supplementary nature of the services. School districts could defeat the program's effort to provide supplementary services to disadvantaged children by reducing the amount of local funds spent on those children. Thus, the federal government developed and/or extended requirements intended to guarantee that (1) local districts maintain their overall levels of spending on education, (2) Title I services to disadvantaged children do not replace similar services that the district previously provided to those students, and (3) districts' per-pupil expenditures in Title I schools are as high as in non-Title I schools.

What has been the effect of these many changes on the consistency of the legal framework? A survey conducted by the Lawyers' Committee for Civil Rights Under Law (Legal Standards Project), concluded that there are no major contradictions in the legal framework.[11] With respect to the formal legal framework, no examples were found of one regulation contradicting another or of one program guideline in conflict with another or with the regulations. Interpretations of the legal framework were also found to be generally consistent, as indicated, for example, by OE correspondence with individual states. Overall, then, Title I regulations, guidelines, and interpretive statements provide the same direction. In addition, the survey found that the legislative and interpretive rules are consistent with "a reasonable interpretation of Congressional intent."[12]

Another characteristic of rule making which may have an impact upon implementation of federal intent is flexibility. A restrictive requirement may be consistent with the legislative intent yet place a burden on the districts that is unnecessary to accomplish the stated policy. Such requirements can impede the development of sound and innovative programs.

Title I does place certain limitations on the allocation of funds. Title I funds must be used to provide services for the intended beneficiaries, and state and local funds must be distributed so that Title I funds actually add to expenditures for the target population. Interviews conducted by NIE, however, revealed that "districts probably would find it difficult to resist the strong pressure to use funds, including those provided through federal programs, for general or emergency needs."[13] Provision of additional services to more affluent areas, use of funds to counter fiscal crises, and development of special programs of a noncompensatory nature are among the unintended uses to which districts might put such funds. Thus, these requirements may be seen as necessary in order to ensure compliance with congressional intent. Furthermore, while the legal framework specifies many conditions for the allocation of funds to schools and students, it allows latitude even in this set of requirements. As described in chapter two, various options and exceptions, as well as loose standards, permit districts considerable discretion in determining who benefits from Title I funds.

With respect to the planning and delivery of services, the framework is even more flexible. Congress has been reluctant to establish requirements in this area, since any restrictions on program delivery are viewed as threats to local control. The legislation does prescribe that the services provided be "of sufficient size, scope, and quality to give reasonable promise of substantial progress." They must also be related to the needs of the students to be served, as well as carefully planned, implemented, and evaluated. Within this broad mandate, districts are permitted a great deal of flexibility. The following examples are all within the range of options permitted by the legal framework.[14]

1. A district may design a Title I program that provides special services to educationally disadvantaged students while they are in their regular classroom (a mainstream program), or it may decide to provide such special instruction in a separate location (a pullout program). The district choosing the latter model may "pull" the student out of the regular classroom for one period or for the entire day and provide a program that is coordinated with regular instruction or restructured in one or more areas of instruction.

2. A district may purchase equipment, materials, and supplies, and even construct buildings with Title I funds under specified conditions, as long as the equipment has been selected and designated for special purposes in connection with a Title I project. Moreover, federal requirements do not prohibit the incidental use of equipment purchased with Title I funds for non-Title I purposes.

3. A district may use Title I funds in any grade; they are not restricted to the elementary grades.

4. A district may use Title I funds to pay for support services, such as psychological counseling or medical assistance, as long as they are shown to be necessary, other sources of funding are not available, and they are not ordinarily provided with state and local funds.

While the rules governing the planning and delivery of services are fairly flexible and represent a common-sense approach to program planning and development, they are not necessary in the sense that the funds allocation requirements are. As Burnes states, "Local districts are not under pressure to deliver bad programs. Nor is there sufficient knowledge about program design and delivery to warrant the mandating of specific procedures or processes."[15] The rules governing program design and implementation neither encourage nor guarantee delivery of high-quality services.

In addition, many of the program development rules are less clear than the funds allocation requirements. According to NIE, states and local districts request clarification of the rules pertaining to program design and implementation far more frequently than they inquire about those governing allocation of funds. Furthermore, many of the conflicts between OE and the states and districts focus on these requirements.

In part, this lack of clarity reflects disagreement within OE about the appropriate federal management role. Those who emphasize service delivery view program quality as a legitimate federal concern; those who support enforcement would limit federal intervention to the prevention of program abuse. Such disagreement has resulted in carefully worded compromises in the rules governing program design and implementation, compromises which fail to provide clear guidance to states and local school districts.

Much of the criticism of the legal framework has pointed to this lack of clarity. NIE notes that "the language of the standards and operational definitions for most LEA program requirements . . . is not sufficiently clear because it does not take into consideration the needs of state and local administrators."[16] Such language can be understood only after extensive study or practical experience. The requirements are neither well written nor sufficiently organized to be self-explanatory.

OE has attempted to improve the clarity of the legal framework by providing individual interpretive responses to state and local queries. According to NIE, many problematic and controversial issues in the legal framework have been addressed in this manner. Such responses typically involve piecemeal interpretations, however. As Burnes observes, "Little attempt has been made to identify the underlying rationale for the rules or the relationship between one rule and several related ones."[17] Nor are the interpretations accompanied by examples which clarify the rules.

Compounding the problem is the fact that these interpretations are not widely or systematically disseminated; they are typically provided only for the state or district making the original inquiry. Not since 1968, when OE published *Program Guide No. 44*, have these interpretations been disseminated in a single, comprehensive document.

The lack of clarity in the federal legal framework is exacerbated by the multiple layers in the administrative system of Title I. In performing their responsibilities for day-to-day oversight of local Title I programs, states must interpret federal policies and provide direction to school districts. States also develop their own policies, which are translated into regulations and guidelines governing local behavior. Failure to comprehend the federal framework may result in inaccurate or illegal state interpretations or in state requirements that are unnecessarily restrictive.

A good illustration of the latter problem concerns the use of pull-out versus mainstream programs. NIE notes that some state educational agencies will not approve mainstream programs, because they perceive pullout programs as the only way to meet the regulations governing the supplementary nature of Title I instruction. Other state educational agencies insist that all Title I instruction be offered in regular classrooms, because they are afraid that pullout programs are generically in violation of the regulations. In fact, the federal rules permit both types of classroom settings.

In 1977 the *DHEW Sanction Study* made a number of recommendations to the Commissioner of Education for improving the clarity of Title I program requirements.[18] These included (1) establishing clear operational definitions for key program requirements in the regulations, (2) publishing examples in the guidelines, (3) maintaining generalized policy statements for some program requirements, and (4) ensuring that additions and refinements which are generated in response to monitoring problems or state/local questions are systematically incorporated into the regulations. Also recommended was more effective communication between OE and state and local agencies, including widespread dissemination of responses to specific inquiries.

In response to a congressional mandate, OE has recently commissioned the development of a comprehensive policy manual for Title I.[19] While this may alleviate the problem, Hill argues that the lack of clarity in the Title I legal framework is inevitable if the rules are to serve as the basis for a formal enforcement system. If this is their purpose, the program rules must be treated as a body of law, for use by legal professionals in formal judicial proceedings. "This requires users of regulations to keep abreast of all recent interpretations and to find all the provisions relevant to [their] case. The possible relationships are as numerous as the numbers of possible cases, i.e., infinite, so the rules cannot possibly be organized to meet the needs of all users."[20]

Whether or not change is possible, the rules governing Title I now resemble a complex code of statutory law and place a heavy burden on users. The result is that states and local school districts often develop varied interpretations of the rules, including some which are overly restrictive.

Monitoring Program

HEW monitors the performance of state and local administrators through annual program reviews conducted by OE's Division of

Education for the Disadvantaged and through occasional formal audits of state and local school districts conducted by the Department of Health, Education, and Welfare's Audit Agency (HEWAA). The difficulties created by the lack of clarity and poor dissemination of Title I rules are compounded in these monitoring efforts.

OE's Title I staff normally monitor the performance of every state educational agency each year. The review is primarily an evaluation of state administration, although visits are also made to a small sample of districts in order to verify state administrative practices. The review team spends approximately ten days in each state, dividing its time between local and state efforts.

The OE review includes both an examination of relevant documents and discussions with state and local officials. Reviewers generally utilize a checklist which covers twelve critical areas of compliance, including fiscal management, comparability, needs assessment, and parent involvement. While in the field, reviewers also provide ad hoc technical assistance in response to requests from state and local officials.

The audits conducted by HEWAA are entirely separate from OE's annual program reviews and are conducted at both state and local levels. Auditors generally look at performance in complying with program requirements and administrative efficiency, as well as fiscal accountability. The audit team, usually consisting of four people, spends from one month to over a year at a site, depending on the size of the program and the complexity of the problems involved. HEWAA does not have sufficient staff to conduct reviews regularly. Selection of cases is based on such factors as requests from various sources (OE staff, the Secretary of HEW, or interested groups), indications of problems, and time elapsed since the last audit.

Based on their findings, auditors make recommendations for procedural changes in administrative practices and for repayment of funds spent in violation of Title I regulations. Once HEWAA issues its findings, OE has the responsibility of determining which findings warrant application of appropriate sanctions. Several levels of OE's bureaucracy are involved in these decisions. When a decision has been made, a final determination letter is sent from OE to the state's chief state school officer. State educational agencies have the right to appeal through the Title I Audit Hearing Board, which comprises both federal employees and individuals from outside the government. The board was established in 1972 to adjudicate disputes arising from the complex issues involved in Title I audits.

These monitoring activities suffer from a number of problems. Perhaps the most serious is the fact that OE officials within apply standards inconsistently as they monitor requirements. NIE examined federal administration of the supplement-not-supplant provisions and found enforcement efforts neither clear nor consistent. Not all program review teams were equally vigorous in monitoring compliance with these requirements, nor did they interpret compliance uniformly. Furthermore, officials at various levels in the OE hierarchy interpreted the provisions differently, with the result that the findings of program review teams were often reversed.

The fact that two separate agencies are responsible for monitoring state and local activities exacerbates this problem. HEWAA frequently disagrees with OE's interpretations of Title I rules. In addition, the agencies disagree over which rules are most important in achieving congressional objectives and which should therefore be singled out for enforcement. Procedures for resolving issues specific to individual audits through arbitration typically entail long delays. Furthermore, there is no mechanism for discussion and resolution of underlying differences in the case of issues which cut across a number of audits or procedural problems.

For the most part, misunderstandings within OE and between OE and HEWAA can be traced back to the lack of clarity in the legal framework. With respect to the supplement-not-supplant provisions, there is disagreement over (1) the standard of measurement (money or services), (2) the level of analysis (state, district, project area, school, or student), (3) the basis of comparison (over time or contemporaneous), (4) the relationship of these provisions to others concerning the use of funds, and (5) the burden of proof (whether it rests with federal or local officials). Without clear rules and operational definitions, determination of compliance is largely based on unofficial guidelines and individual interpretations, not on regulations. Such informal guidelines provide a very shaky foundation for federal management.

Inconsistency in the federal monitoring of regulations reinforces the unnecessarily restrictive interpretations adopted by some state and local officials. It also encourages agencies and districts to seek out federal officials who provide policy interpretations consistent with state and local practice.[21] An even more serious consequence of inconsistency, however, is the gradual erosion of federal oversight and enforcement efforts.

According to NIE, controversy surrounding enforcement of the supplement-not-supplant provisions has resulted in fewer allegations of noncompliance, recommendations for less severe corrective action, and limited application of formal sanctions even in the most clear-cut instances of noncompliance. It has also resulted in a significant decline in monitoring activity on the part of both OE and HEWAA staff. Thus, states and districts now receive little clear guidance and minimal supervision with respect to this essential feature of the Title I program.

The lack of clarity and consistency in federal direction is reflected in the role of the states in monitoring district performance. Primary responsibility for local oversight rests with the states, which are supposed to make regular, systematic inspections of district practices and ensure that each district is audited at least every two years. Despite the importance of the state role, the federal legal framework has no clear requirements concerning the nature and extent of state monitoring and no established guidelines for the conduct of state audits. State sanctioning authority is even more ambiguous; it is not clear whether states have the authority to withhold or suspend funds.

This lack of clarity is reflected in varying attitudes toward state enforcement of federal rules. Some states, valuing local autonomy, play a rather passive role in monitoring Title I programs in their districts; others monitor local programs closely. The result is that in some states fewer than 5 percent of the local districts may be visited in a year, while in others nearly half may be observed.[22]

Thus, in addition to clarification of the law, successful federal management of Title I requires improved monitoring efforts. OE and HEWAA must adopt consistent policies and agree upon a single interpretation of basic rules. In view of the significant differences among states in their commitment to local oversight, additional rules as well as incentives may be necessary to guarantee that all states meet their monitoring responsibilities.

Enforcement of Rules

HEW has two separate enforcement systems, each of which is linked to one of the monitoring activities described above. If an OE program review team concludes that state or local plans are out of compliance with the regulations, a series of actions is initiated. Upon approval by the Associate Commissioner for Compensatory Education Programs, reports and recommendations are sent to the state's chief state school officer. Where changes are deemed necessary, the state is expected to submit a written reply within sixty days, outlining the corrective action it will undertake. If the problems identified by the review team are serious and the state refuses to alter its policies or procedures, a hearing process is initiated. The state application may be rejected and Title I funds withheld if the state fails to make its case during the hearing.

This form of sanction is rarely utilized, in part because monitoring activities are too superficial to uncover any but the most blatant cases of noncompliance. Nor is noncompliance generally uncovered during the program application process, since completing the state application is generally a perfunctory matter. In recent years only California has submitted a noncompliant state application, and this was done intentionally in order to bring to light a conflict between Title I and a state categorical aid program. When OE threatened to suspend Title I funds in the state, California submitted a revised application, which was accepted.

A second form of sanction may be employed as a result of the audit process. If an audit team discovers evidence of past misuse of funds, it estimates the amount of illegal expenditure. After a complicated review process, OE is responsible for making final determinations and collecting misspent funds from the responsible state or local agency.

Although HEWAA is fairly aggressive in its enforcement efforts, this complex administrative review process often delays and impedes the recovery of funds. As Hill points out, the "process invites the formation of strong state-local-Congressional coalitions in an effort to excuse the district from having to return funds. As a result, [HEWAA's] findings are frequently reversed or watered down."[23] HEW statistics support Hill's contention. Between 1965 and 1975 $259 million in Title I expenditures were questioned or recommended for refund by HEWAA. OE requested that $12 million of that amount be reimbursed, yet as of January, 1977, only $1 million had been refunded.[24]

Both sanctions suffer from the draconian nature of the penalties imposed for noncompliance. As Burnes observes, "A minor infraction of the regulations in one school building can jeopardize an entire district's Title I grant for a considerable period of time."[25] Furthermore, both the withholding of current funds and the collection of misspent funds typically result in the interruption of services to those for whom the funds are intended. Thus, OE has strong incentives not to apply these sanctions.

Less severe sanctions and changes in administrative procedures have been proposed, including a lag between the identification of an infraction and the demand for repayment. Currently, however, it is the threat of such sanctions, rather than the penalties, which encourages compliance with federal intent.

THE INFORMAL MANAGEMENT SYSTEM

The formal management system emerges from and is designed to enforce the legislative rules governing Title I. In addition to formal management, the federal government employs a number of informal strategies to influence state and local behavior. These are built upon the informal linkages which exist among federal, state, and local Title I officials. Furthermore, pressures for compliance exist because of the interests federal administrators share with Title I parents and advocacy groups. Essentially, informal management of Title I rests upon three factors: (1) professional ties among federal, state, and local administrators, (2) informal incentives and sanctions which exist within and among intergovernmental levels, and (3) the efforts of private citizens.

Professional Ties

Federal, state, and local administrators of Title I form an informal network of professionals. Title I is totally funded by the federal government and typically administered by special staff within the state or local educational agencies. Hill notes that the "expertise [of these individuals] —and thus their professional standing—is based on the distinctiveness of the programs they manage."[26] Efforts by state and local agencies to utilize Title I funds for purposes of general aid or tax relief are met with a certain amount of resistance by such officials.

It should be pointed out that the recent proliferation and expansion of state compensatory programs may begin to erode these professional ties. In many cases, the administration of state compensatory programs is handled by the same professionals who oversee Title I administration. To the extent that federal and state policies and practices are consistent, such pooling of staff need not impede compliance with federal requirements. Where federal and state goals are in conflict, however, the natural professional alliance between federal and state officials may be weakened.

Informal Incentives and Sanctions

A number of informal incentives facilitate compliance with Title I.
OE has publicly commended several districts for their "sound and
innovative" programs. In addition, districts with promising Title I
programs may be rewarded by having their programs packaged and
disseminated nationally. Perhaps the strongest incentive, however, is
the desire for professional recognition by colleagues.

Informal sanctions also exist. For example, while few districts are
audited or reviewed in any given year, the threat of such actions
serves as a sanction. A lower level of government (for example, a district) is typically concerned about criticism of administrative performance coming from a higher level (for example, a state educational agency). Also, allegations of misuse of funds open state and local
Title I staff to criticism by the press.

For these informal incentives and sanctions to be effective, information concerning the adequacy of state and local performance
must be available. In a sense, then, the evaluation requirements in the
Title I legal framework, which mandate state and local assessment of
student progress in meeting program objectives, are also elements of
the informal management system.

Efforts of Private Citizens

At every level of government different groups support the goals of
Title I. Many are general advocacy groups, such as community action
agencies, civil rights groups, minority group caucuses, and welfare beneficiaries' associations. In addition, Title I requires the establishment
of district- and school-level parent advisory councils. Members of
these groups have a personal stake in ensuring that Title I funds are
not abused. Such groups have three avenues by which to exert pressure for compliance. First, they can apply direct pressure on the
agency involved. If the state or local education agency is perceived to
be misusing funds, for example, citizens may attempt to bring about
compliance through communication and persuasion. Second, if ac-
commodation is not possible through direct communication, such
groups have recourse within the formal management structure. The
legal framework sets forth a detailed set of procedures to handle
complaints by private citizens. Finally, if satisfaction is not received
within the delivery system per se, pressure groups can resort to court
action to bring about compliance.

Pressure groups exist at all levels in the educational delivery system. Perhaps the most influential thus far are national advocacy groups, which have succeeded in changing portions of both the legal framework and the formal management system. In selected instances, national advocacy groups have also wielded tremendous power over state and local agencies. [27]

Local parent advisory councils have not exerted as much pressure for compliance as have these other groups. In part, this stems from lack of clarity in the legal framework concerning council functions; in part it is the result of failure by state and local Title I officials to give the advisory councils a meaningful governance role. As both Murphy and Hill point out, however, such groups have enormous power to facilitate compliance, if this power can be properly mobilized. [28]

SUMMARY AND CONCLUSIONS

The legal framework of Title I is generally content and flexible enough to allow the development of sound, innovative educational programs. Yet the rules are not sufficiently clear nor interpretations of them well enough disseminated to prevent ambiguity and unnecessarily restrictive behavior from being adopted. Furthermore, there are serious problems with current monitoring and enforcement activities. Monitoring is inconsistent, and sanctions are extreme and disruptive in nature. The informal management system has several components, at least one of which—parental pressure—has not yet been fully utilized.

Despite all these problems, there is evidence that compliance with federal requirements has been increasing over the years. An OE analysis of audits and program reviews revealed that compliance with Title I program requirements improved from 1971 to 1974. OE identifies twelve critical program areas and rates the performance of state educational agencies on a scale from 0 percent to 100 percent, with 60 percent indicating satisfactory performance. From 1971 to 1974 the average state compliance rose form 39 to 63 percent, a significant improvement. HEWAA also conducted a fourteen-state survey comparing each state's 1972-73 management performance with similar data for the 1969-70 school year. Use of Title I funds for general aid declined substantially during that period. More recently NIE found an overall pattern of compliance, as noted in the following excerpt from the Senate Report on the Education Amendments of 1978:

> The first major conclusion of the [NIE] study is that Title I is successful
> in directing substantial Federal aid to those areas which have the high-

est proportions of children from low-income families. Although Title I funds constitute less than 5 percent of all national expenditures for elementary and secondary education, Title I often accounts for one-sixth of the funding in the very poorest school districts. In addition, the Institute found that Title I has greater redistributive effect than other State and Federal aid-to-education programs. Title I allocated more than 5½ times as much aid per pupil to the districts with the highest poverty rates as to the lowest. Title I also provides slightly more money to districts with small local tax bases than to districts which are able to provide high levels of local spending.

At the school building level, data from evaluations funded by the Office of Education indicate that schools which receive Title I funds tend to have high concentrations of students from poverty background and high concentrations of poor readers.[29]

While each of the components of the federal administrative structure is imperfect, together they provide strong direction and support for federal policy. The legal framework, despite its imperfections, does provide a reference point for both formal and informal management systems. However, lack of clarity and spotty dissemination often result in unnecessarily restrictive behavior on the part of state and local agencies. The difficult task facing federal administrators is to provide guidelines and operational definitions which are not overly restrictive. The other aspects of the formal management structure also have limitations, with the result that sanctions are almost never applied. Yet oversight and the *threat* of sanctions underly the success of the informal management structure. Pressures from state and local officials, and from the general public, when coupled with judicial review, help ensure conformity with federal policy.

Notes

1.   See Murphy, "Title I of ESEA," pp. 35-63; Peter G. Briggs, *A Perspective on Change: The Administration of Title I of the Elementary and Secondary Education Act* (Washington, D.C.: The Planar Corp., October 1973); Joel S. Berke and Michael W. Kirst, eds., *Federal Aid to Education: Who Benefits? Who Governs?* (Lexington, Mass.: Lexington Books, 1973); and Charles L. Blaschke, *Dysfunctional Elements in the Governance of ESEA Title I: Why Successful Programs are Often Illegal* (September 1976).

2.   In *A Perspective on Change* Briggs distinguishes between management (planning, organizing, directing, and controlling) and administration (directing and, to a lesser extent, controlling). We use the term management hereafter to refer to the broadest possible set of functions which could be performed.

3.   Bailey and Mosher, *ESEA: The Office of Education Administers a Law,* p. 50.

4.   Michael Kirst, "Delivery Systems for Federal Aid to Disadvantaged Children," (Palo Alto, Calif.: Stanford University, 1972), p. 17.

5.   See Paul Berman and Milbrey McLaughlin, *Federal Programs Supporting Educational Change,* vol. I, *A Model of Educational Change* (Santa Monica, Calif.: Rand Corporation, 1975); and Sheila Rosenblum and Karen Seashore Louis, *A Measure of Change: The Process and Outcomes of Planned Change in Ten Rural School Districts* (Cambridge, Mass.: Abt Associates Inc., October 1978).

6.   Berman and McLaughlin, *Federal Programs Supporting Educational Change,* vol. I.

7.   Paul T. Hill, "Enforcement and Informal Pressure in the Management of Federal Categorical Programs in Education" (draft) (Washington, D.C.: Rand Corporation, December 1978), p. 2.

8.   This chapter relies on existing research literature; it is not supported by any new data. Discussion of the formal management system draws heavily from the NIE report to Congress, *Administration of Compensatory Education* and from Donald W. Burnes, "A Case Study of Federal Involvement in Education," *Proceedings of the Academy of Political Science* 33, no. 2 (1978): 88-98. Discussion of the informal management system relies primarily upon Hill, "Enforcement and Informal Pressure."

9.   NAACP Legal Defense and Education Fund, *Title I in Your Community,* (New York: NAACP, 1971); Murphy, *Title I of ESEA.*

10.   Hill, "Enforcement and Informal Pressure."

11.   The complete findings of this survey are contained in four separate volumes. See NIE, *Administration of Compensatory Education.*

12.   Ibid., p. 13.

13.   Ibid.

14.   These examples were derived from a review of the statutes and regulations and were generally contained in OE interpretations to the districts. See NIE, *Administration of Compensatory Education,* pp. 19-21.

15.   Burnes, "A Case Study," p. 91.

16.   NIE, *Administration of Compensatory Education,* p. 17.

17. Burnes, "A Case Study," p. 91.

18. Office of the Assistant Secretary of Education/Policy Development, *DHEW Sanction Study* (Washington, D.C.: U.S. Department of Health, Education, and Welfare, January 1977).

19. This is presently being developed by Educational Turnkey Systems, Inc. with Abt Associates Inc. and Simon, Deitch, Roth, Siefman, and Tucker under contract to OE.

20. Hill, "Enforcement and Informal Pressure," p. 10.

21. Martin E. Orland, Robert Goettel, and Bernard Kaplan, "A Study of the Administration of ESEA, Title I at the Federal, State and Local Level: A Final Report" (draft) (Syracuse: Syracuse Research Corporation, June 1977).

22. Burnes, "A Case Study."

23. Hill, "Enforcement and Informal Pressure," p. 16.

24. *DHEW Sanction Study.*

25. Burnes, "A Case Study," p. 96.

26. Hill, "Enforcement and Informal Pressure," p. 19.

27. In chapter nine we describe the instrumental role of one such group in forcing one of the sixteen original demonstration districts to drop out of the study.

28. Murphy, "Title I of ESEA"; and Hill, "Enforcement and Informal Pressure."

29. *Report on the Educational Amendments of 1978,* p. 7.

===== 4 =====

Distributive Equity and the School and Student Selection Process

Federal regulations require a two-stage process for selecting the beneficiaries of Title I services. First, schools are identified as eligible on
the basis of economic criteria. Second, students are selected in eligible
schools on the basis of educational need. In this chapter we describe
the criteria and procedures employed in the selection process, using
data from NIE's national survey, supplemented by data from the
thirteen demonstration districts.[1] We also attempt to assess the equity
of the process by describing the schools and students served under
current Title I regulations in the demonstration districts.

THE SELECTION PROCESS IN PRACTICE
Before considering issues of equity, it is useful to examine how school
districts actually go about selecting the schools and the students who
are served by Title I programs.

School Eligibility and Targeting
According to NIE's national survey, school districts employ various
poverty measures to determine which schools are eligible for Title I

funds. The three sources of information on poverty most commonly used by districts in 1975-76 to identify eligible schools were 1970 census data in conjunction with the Orshansky poverty index (used by 67 percent of the districts surveyed), counts of free lunch recipients (used by 66 percent of the districts surveyed), and current AFDC counts (used by 51 percent of the districts surveyed).[2] At least seven other information sources were used occasionally, including public housing statistics, unemployment records, and district surveys of economic need. The percentages total more than 100 because many districts employ more than one source of data to determine school eligibility.[3]

The regulations allow districts to choose from among several measures of poverty on the assumption that no single data source is generally available; NIE's survey results confirm this belief. In some areas county welfare offices are apparently unwilling to help district administrators determine the number of children in AFDC families on a school-by-school basis. Therefore, AFDC data cannot always be used. In addition, 1970 census data are available only for large districts, and even they have turned to other data sources as the census has become outdated. Large urban districts are more likely than others to use AFDC counts or their own poverty surveys rather than census data in determining school eligibility.[4] In general, the number of free lunch recipients is the most readily available source of poverty data for most school districts.

NIE's survey data indicate that a very high proportion (68 percent) of the schools in Title I districts were classified as eligible. That rate of eligibility is far higher than it would be if only one eligibility criterion were applied. Using census, AFDC, or free lunch data alone, the average district could identify no more than 48 percent of its schools as eligible for Title I.[5] It appears therefore that districts tend to select that criterion or combination of criteria which maximizes the number of eligible schools.

Other factors which might explain the large percentage of schools deemed eligible include the thirty percent and formerly eligible exceptions described in chapter two. Since these requirements had been in effect for barely a year when NIE's survey was conducted, however, it seems unlikely that either would explain the large percentage of eligible schools. Nor does the no wide variance exception (which would permit a district to identify all its attendance areas as eligible) help to explain this percentage.[6]

NIE's survey revealed considerable variability in what is required to determine a "concentration" of poor children. Since school eligibility is a function of the district's average number or percent of children from low-income families, the schools that qualify can vary considerably with respect to this criterion. One district in NIE's survey had so few poor children that an attendance area was counted eligible when only 2 percent of its children were from low-income families. In a much poorer district, 77 percent of the children had to be disadvantaged for the school to be eligible.

In theory, the process of school targeting is distinct from determination of eligibility. To prevent spreading Title I resources too thinly, the regulations encourage districts to limit the number of eligible schools that actually receive Title I services. In fact, however, school targeting as a separate step is practically nonexistent. Over 80 percent of Title I districts report serving all eligible schools, and 94 percent of eligible schools are targeted for Title I services.[7] Thus, there is little variation in district selection, and most eligible schools are targeted. Overall, some 62 percent of all schools in Title I districts receive some Title I services.

Student Eligibility and Targeting

Less is known about the manner in which students are deemed eligible and targeted for service within Title I schools. Data from the thirteen demonstration districts suggest that criteria and procedures vary widely from district to district and within districts.

In 1975-76, the baseline year for the demonstration, program administrators in each of these school systems reported using a variety of tests in determining student eligibility for Title I. In some instances, the tests were administered following a set of screening activities: only students who had been served previously, had poor grades, or were referred by their teachers were tested to ascertain their eligibility for Title I. In many cases, informal checklists, as well as judgments by teachers, principals, and parents, were used to add to the pool of students deemed eligible on the basis of test scores alone.

The specific tests varied among districts and by subject area and grade level within districts. While most employed standardized achievement tests, one district developed its own criterion-referenced tests (that is, tests oriented specifically to the program's objectives) to assess student achievement. In addition, the cutoff points below which a student was deemed eligible varied considerably from one district to another and from one subject and grade level to the next. In some districts students scoring below the 50th percentile on a standardized test of achievement qualified for Title I, whereas in one district only students scoring below the 23rd percentile were deemed eligible.

All districts reported targeting students on the basis of educational need, with those most in need served first. Few defined need solely on the basis of test scores, however. In most cases, the judgment of staff and parents played a major role in the identification of those students to be served.

QUESTIONS OF EQUITY IN THE DISTRIBUTION OF RESOURCES

Within the context of this chapter, equity can be understood in two different ways. *Vertical equity* is defined by the extent to which those schools or students most in need of Title I services are selected to receive them. According to the legal framework of Title I, the schools or students having the greatest need are to be selected first, with subsequent selection based on diminishing degrees of need until resources are exhausted. For a given level of resources, a state of perfect vertical equity is one in which *only* the neediest schools or students receive Title I services.

Vertical equity and vertical inequity are illustrated in Figure 4-1, which shows differing degrees of concentration of Title I resources among students within a school. Where perfect vertical equity prevails, there is a sharp distinction between Title I and non-Title I students based on achievement level: only low achievers are served. However, perfect vertical equity does not require that *all* low achievers be served. Funding constraints may require a cutoff line; low achievers above that line will not receive services. But as long as the neediest of the group of eligible students are served, there is vertical equity. In the case of vertical inequity, the distribution of Title I resources is random with respect to achievement. Both low-achieving students (in this illustration, those reading one or more years below grade level) and other students receive Title I services.

The other kind of equity which interests us is *horizontal equity*. There is horizontal equity when schools or students having equal needs also have equal chances of receiving Title I services. Perfect vertical equity, as depicted in Figure 4-1, necessarily implies perfect horizontal equity. At any given level of educational need, every student has the same chance of being selected for Title I. For all levels of achievement below the cutoff line, every student's chance is 100 per-

FIGURE 4-1. VERTICAL EQUITY AND INEQUITY IN DISTRIBUTION OF
TITLE I SERVICES TO STUDENTS

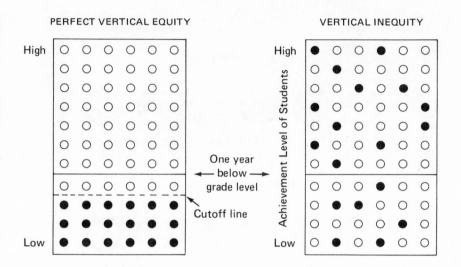

KEY
● Student receiving Title I services
○ Student not receiving Title I services

cent; for all levels above the line, each student's chance is zero. This means that horizontal inequities come into play only when vertical inequities exist. Since a student's chances of being selected at a given level of educational need are less than 100 percent or greater than zero, the distribution of resources at that level can be either equitable or inequitable, depending on whether or not each student's chances at that level are identical.

While vertical equity can be determined strictly in terms of results (concentration of resources among the lowest-achieving students), horizontal equity can only be inferred from results. The fact that some low-achieving students receive Title I services and others do not has no implications for horizontal equity unless there is evidence of bias in the selection process. In this respect, horizontal inequity may resemble discrimination based on race or sex.

Figure 4-2 contrasts hypothetical cases of horizontal equity and inequity. In both cases, only three of the six low-achieving students

FIGURE 4-2. HORIZONTAL EQUITY AND INEQUITY IN DISTRIBUTION
OF TITLE I SERVICES TO STUDENTS

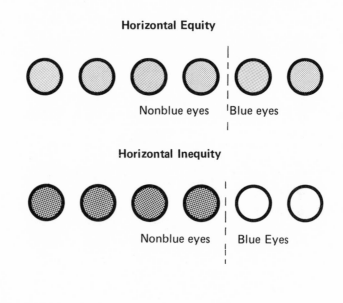

Horizontal Equity

Nonblue eyes   ¦Blue eyes

Horizontal Inequity

Nonblue eyes   ¦ Blue Eyes

KEY

◯ Student with a 50% chance of being selected for Title I.

◉ Student with a 75% chance of being selected for Title I.

◯ Student with zero chance of being selected for Title I.

will be chosen to receive Title I services. In the example of horizontal equity, each low-achieving student has a 50 percent chance of receiving Title I services, regardless of eye color. In the case of horizontal inequity, two of the six low-achieving students are discriminated against on the basis of eye color. Those with blue eyes have no chance of being selected for Title I programs, the rest have a seventy-five percent chance. The applicability of these concepts to the selection process used in the Title I program will become clear in succeeding sections of this chapter.

SCHOOL SELECTION OUTCOMES

In formal terms, districts always achieve perfect vertical equity in their selection of Title I schools, since by definition only "poor" schools are eligible for Title I services, and the poorest are served first. Using their own definitions of eligibility, the districts also come close to achieving perfect horizontal equity: because there is so little targeting, each eligible school has almost a 100 percent chance of being selected for service. However, school districts tailor their definitions of poverty to their own purposes and to available data, as they are permitted to do by law. The result is that the same school might be selected for Title I services by one district but not by another. How much equity would we find if we used some standard criterion of poverty, rather than many variable ones?

As noted above, the measures of povery most commonly used by school districts in their selection of Title I schools are the proportion of students classified as poor on the basis of the Orshansky poverty index, the proportion from AFDC families, and the proportion receiving free lunches. The particular ways in which these and other measures are used, either singly or in combination, to classify schools for selection purposes vary from district to district. However, once they have arrived at a definition of poverty-level students, districts follow a standard procedure. Each district calculates the number or proportion of such students districtwide. Any school which has a number or proportion of poor students higher than the districtwide proportion is eligible to receive Title I funds.

Let us see which of the various poverty measures best discriminates between Title I and non-Title I schools. Table 4-1, derived from baseline data in the thirteen demonstration districts, shows the difference between Title I and non-Title I schools in the proportion of low-income third and fourth graders in each site, as measured by three different criteria. The percentage of poor students is almost uniformly higher in Title I than in non-Title I schools. However, although there is considerable variability from district to district, the average differences are not striking. Using the free lunch criterion, the mean difference is 22 percent; using the poverty threshold of the Orshansky poverty index, it is 13 percent; and using AFDC status, it is only 6 percent.[8]

If free lunch status were to be regarded as an "objective" measure of poverty in a district, how many Title I and non-Title I schools would have to be reclassified? That is, how many non-Title I schools

TABLE 4-1. PERCENT DIFFERENCE BETWEEN TITLE I AND NON-TITLE I
SCHOOLS IN PROPORTIONS OF LOW-INCOME STUDENTS ACCORDING
TO THREE MEASURES OF POVERTY

DISTRICTS	FREE LUNCH PARTICIPATION	ORSHANSKY POVERTY INDEX	AFDC STATUS
Adams County #12	10%*	14%	3%
Alum Rock	19*	9	20*
Berkeley County	14*	−12	6
Boston	25*	20*	5
Charlotte	11*	13*	4
Harrison County	25*	23	5
Houston	41*	23*	5*
Mesa	14*	−1	5*
Newport	22*	——	——
Racine	13*	4	1
Santa Fe	33*	44*	2
Winston-Salem	8*	4	2
Yonkers	57*	31*	16*
Mean	22	14	6

*p < .05

Note: Small sample sizes in Newport precluded inclusion of AFDC and poverty
data.

would have proportions of poor children higher than the districtwide
proportion, and how many Title I schools would have proportions
lower than the districtwide proportion?

In each demonstration district we can compute the proportion of
third- and fourth-grade free lunch students in every sample school
and compare these school figures with the districtwide proportion. In
so doing, we find that an average of 31 percent of the non-Title I
schools in these districts would qualify for Title I programs if free
lunch status were the sole criterion for school selection. Furthermore,
the deviation of these non-Title I schools above districtwide proportions is fairly substantial—an average difference of 17 percent. On the

other side, almost one-quarter (24 percent) of the Title I schools would not qualify, using the free lunch criterion. In this case, however, average difference would be smaller—8 percent. Thus, in a typical demonstration district, where about 38 percent of all third and fourth graders would be classified as poor by the free lunch criterion, about one-third of the non-Title I schools had an average proportion of 55 percent poor children, while around one-quarter of the Title I schools had an average proportion of 30 percent poor children.

By the free lunch criterion, then, there would be a substantial amount of vertical inequity in the school selection process, because Title I resources would be going to nonpoor schools, while being denied to poor schools.[9] We could draw no conclusions about horizontal equity because we would have no way of ascertaining whether equally poor schools had equal chances of being selected.

These findings do not reveal that the demonstration districts have misclassified large numbers of schools. As observed above, school districts are allowed to select among measures (or use a combination of them) in defining poverty status for the purpose of selecting schools. What the calculations illustrate is that the use of alternative and quite reasonable poverty criteria can result in fairly large numbers of schools either being included or excluded, with important consequences for the children in these schools. Hence, the notion that in each district there is a clearly definable block of disadvantaged schools requiring Title I assistance seems questionable.

What are the consequences of federal rules governing school selection and district-specific selection procedures for the selection of low-achieving students in Title I schools? The use of poverty-based school criteria to determine which schools receive Title I funds assumes a correlation between a school's concentration of low-income and low-achieving students. How accurate is this assumption; that is, how efficient is poverty-based school selection in identifying schools with high proportions of low-achieving students?

Wolf summarized a number of studies relating school achievement data to information on free lunch and welfare counts. According to the author, "the results suggest that the correlation between the poverty of a district's schools and their achievement is high in areas where the economic differences are extreme, and where the contrast in the average family background of pupils in different schools tends to be correspondingly marked."[10] Thus, high correlations are found in large urban districts where neighborhoods tend to be both internally homogeneous and different from one another. Summarizing data collected by various researchers in nine urban centers, the author reports correlations ranging from .7 to .9, with most above .8.

In other areas, where housing is less economically segregated or where desegregation has changed school attendance patterns, however, the relationship is less close and shows wide variation. In the demonstration districts, for example (which are primarily newer, non-urban communities and which in many cases have recently undergone desegregation), the correlation between the percentage of children receiving free lunch and a school's mean reading level averaged .58. However, there was enormous variation. In two districts the correlations exceeded .7, but in five (including a large desegregated city) they were below .5, and in one there was little relationship.

The proportion of low achievers in Title I schools is also a measure of the efficiency of current school selection procedures. To obtain a measure of achievement, we asked third- and fourth-grade teachers in all sample schools in the thirteen demonstration districts to rate the reading achievement of each of their students on a five-point scale: (1) more than one year behind grade level, (2) one year behind grade level, (3) one-half year behind grade level, (4) at grade level, and (5) above grade level.[11] Low achievers were defined as those reading one year or more below grade level. It should be emphasized that this measure is quite conservative and does not represent the actual cutoff levels defined by the demonstration districts. Albeit somewhat arbitrary, this criterion was the one adopted by Congress for purposes of research.[12]

Table 4-2 shows the percentage of elementary schools served by each district during 1975-76, as well as the estimated percentage of all third- and fourth-grade low achievers in the district who attended these schools. On the average, the demonstration districts served 50 percent of their elementary schools, although the range varied from 19 to 83 percent. Approximately 55 percent of the low-achieving third and fourth graders attended these schools with the range being equally widespread. Thus, in selecting half of their Title I schools, districts usually served over half of their low-achieving students.

These data support the hypothesis that poverty may be a reasonable surrogate for low achievement, at least at the school level. However, they also dramatize the fact that current school selection procedures result in relatively large proportions of low-achieving students being denied access to services based solely on residence area. This does not necessarily suggest that other school selection methods

**TABLE 4-2. PERCENTAGE OF ELEMENTARY SCHOOLS SERVED
AND PERCENTAGE OF ALL THIRD- AND FOURTH-GRADE
LOW ACHIEVERS IN TITLE I SCHOOLS, 1975-76**

DISTRICTS	PERCENTAGE OF ALL THIRD- AND FOURTH-GRADE LOW ACHIEVERS IN TITLE I SCHOOLS	PERCENTAGE OF ELEMENTARY SCHOOLS SERVED
Adams County #12	22%	19%
Alum Rock	52	47
Berkeley County	69	77
Boston	69	56
Charlotte	69	67
Harrison County	83	83
Houston	36	32
Mesa	58	56
Newport	37	33
Racine	37	48
Santa Fe	77	69
Winston-Salem	39	35
Yonkers	62	29
Mean	55	50

are more efficient in defining large pools of low-achieving students. Evidence for the relative efficiency of other methods of school selection is presented in chapter seven.

STUDENT SELECTION OUTCOMES

As noted earlier, the legal framework requires that students be selected on the basis of educational need, beginning with those whose need is greatest, and continuing with those who have less need, until resources are exhausted. In theory, these requirements necessarily imply a sharp dividing line between Title I and non-Title I students, a cutoff which is reached when the students with the greatest need have been selected and no more resources remain. Whether actual student selection procedures result in such sharp distinctions is the question addressed here.

Baseline data from the thirteen demonstration districts enable us to assess the extent of vertical equity within Title I schools. Table 4-3 shows the percentages of third and fourth graders at each of five reading achievement levels who are enrolled in Title I schools and who have been selected for Title I. The lowest two categories (one year below grade level and more than one year below grade level) correspond to an early congressional definition of low achievers.

There is a strong relation between reading level and the probability of selection for Title I in most of the districts. As reading level increases, the probability of selection decreases substantially. However, not all students at a given reading level are served before students at the next level are selected for services, as would be the case if perfect vertical equity existed. Indeed, in Alum Rock, where 85 percent of the students are classified by the district as educationally disadvantaged for purposes of federal and state reporting, Title I services are distributed rather evenly among students. Thus, making allowances for problems of definition and measurement error, it seems reasonable to conclude that the demonstration districts strive for vertical equity but do not fully succeed in achieving it.

Apparent vertical inequity may result from the introduction into the student selection process of data other than achievement test scores. While the rules governing local behavior demand that students be served on the basis of educational deprivation, districts are given broad latitude in determining educational need. In addition, vertical equity may be related to concentration and resource allocation decisions. For example, a district seeking to concentrate all of its resources in a limited number of schools might use a very liberal achievement cutoff line and pay little attention to targeting students within Title I schools. In contrast, a district seeking to distribute resources among many schools would be forced to use a more restrictive cutoff line and be more selective in student targeting. As noted in the introduction, the distribution of resources among schools in a district may also vary. Schools receiving more resources relative to the number of low-achieving students might adopt a less selective targeting policy than others.

The appearance of vertical inequities in the student selection process suggests the possibility that horizontal inequities may also be present. Horizontal inequities result from some bias in the selection process such that equally disadvantaged students do not have equal

TABLE 4-3. PERCENTAGE OF STUDENTS IN TITLE I SCHOOLS SELECTED FOR SERVICE BY READING ACHIEVEMENT LEVEL, 1975-76

	READING ACHIEVEMENT LEVEL				
Districts	More Than 1 Year Below Grade Level	1 Year Below Grade Level	1/2 Year Below Grade Level	At Grade Level	Above Grade Level
Adams County #12	48%	13%	5%	.2%	0%
Alum Rock	50	54	53	55	46
Berkeley County	42	33	15	3	3
Boston	74	67	45	19	6
Charlotte	77	52	25	3	1
Harrison County	81	65	33	4	.6
Houston	58	55	44	23	12
Mesa	73	57	38	21	8
Newport	52	62	39	15	4
Racine	44	34	17	1	0
Santa Fe	80	55	36	6	3
Winston-Salem	84	67	44	5	0
Yonkers	90	82	80	67	37
Mean	66	54	36	17	9

chances of being chosen for Title I. To address the question of horizontal equity, we examine the extent to which other factors are related to Title I selection after achievement levels are taken into account.

Using data from our student rosters, we can determine whether being selected a Title I student within a Title I school is related to economic status (as measured by free lunch participation), minority status, or sex. To do this, we predict Title I status for students in Title I schools as a function of these three variables and of reading achievement (measured on our five-point scale). Table 4-4, which presents the regression results for each demonstration district, shows how the probability of being selected for Title I is related to each of these variables.[13]

Reading achievement is clearly the most important of the four determinants of Title I status considered here. The coefficients for reading achievement are statistically significant in all but one of the districts, and the average coefficient is –.14. This means that, on the average, as reading level *decreases* one step—say from a half to a full year below grade level—the probability of a student being selected for Title I *increases* by 14 percent. Moving the full four steps down the reading achievement scale increases a student's chances by 56 percent.[14]

Economic status, as measured by participation in a free lunch program, is a significant factor in eight of the thirteen districts, but the coefficients are generally much smaller than those for reading achievement. On the average, participating in a free lunch program increases a student's chances of being included in a Title I program by only 3 percent. There are some striking exceptions, however. In Newport, Houston, and Yonkers, there is a strong relationship between economic status and Title I selection; low-income students have a 19 percent to 27 percent better chance of being chosen for a Title I program, even when reading achievement, race, and sex are held constant.

The interpretation of a free lunch effect on Title I status as a bias in selection depends on one's philosophy of compensatory education and the corresponding definition of appropriate student populations to be served. As we have seen, although poverty status plays the primary role in school selection, Title I regulations demand that only achievement be considered in determining student eligibility. Concern over this lack of consideration of poverty status at the student level has been expressed by educators as well as in congressional delibera-

TABLE 4-4. DETERMINANTS OF TITLE I STATUS WITHIN TITLE I SCHOOLS (REGRESSION COEFFICIENTS) 1975-76*

	DETERMINANTS			
DISTRICTS (N)	READING ACHIEVEMENT (5-point scale)	FREE LUNCH (1 = Y) (0 = N)	MINORITY STATUS (1 = nonwhite 0 = white)	SEX (1 = male 0 = female)
Adams County #12 (509)	-.10**	.01	.05	.00
Alum Rock (1,790)	.00	.01	.09	.00
Berkeley County (1,131)	-.10**	.02	.04	.02
Boston (5,674)	-.17**	.01	.05**	.00
Charlotte (7,769)	-.19**	.04**	.08**	.03
Harrison County (1,905)	-.24**	.07**	.09**	.03
Houston (9,747)	-.10**	.24**	.00	.09**
Mesa (1,911)	-.16**	.03**	.02	.04
Newport (191)	-.15**	.19**	-.16**	.15**
Racine (1,415)	-.12**	-.02	.02	.00
Santa Fe (1,190)	-.19**	.11**	-.02	-.02
Winston-Salem (2,243)	-.23**	.03**	.02	.00
Yonkers (720)	-.06**	.27**	.24**	.06
Mean	-.14	.08	.04	.03

*A negative sign indicates that the better the reader, the less likely she or he is to receive Title I services.

**p ≤ .05

tions on revisions to the allocation formulas. Poverty status has, for example, been suggested as a student eligibility criterion to be used in conjunction with student achievement. This aspect of the poverty/achievement debate is certainly not settled.

Minority status as a factor in selection is related to Title I status in six of the thirteen districts. However, on the average, being a member of a minority group increases the probability of being selected by only a little over 4 percent. Again there are interesting exceptions. A minority student in Yonkers has a 24 percent chance of being in a Title I program than a white student, while in Newport being white increases a student's chances by 16 percent after the other factors are taken into account.

Sex is the least important of the four factors related to Title I status. In only three of the thirteen districts does sex have a significant relationship; in all the rest the coefficients are below 3 percent.

In Alum Rock selection seems to have no significant relation to a student's reading ability, economic status, or sex, but membership in a minority group increases a student's chances by 9 percent. This is not surprising considering that 85 percent of Alum Rock's elementary school students are educationally disadvantaged according to district criteria. Serving all low achievers in Alum Rock may thus imply serving all elementary school students in the district.

These results suggest that the districts attempt to achieve horizontal equity in the selection process, although some factors other than achievement level are utilized. In most cases low economic status and minority status increase a student's chances by small but significant amounts, although in three districts—Houston, Newport, and Yonkers—these factors are closely related to selection. Sex appears to be unrelated to student selection once other factors are controlled.

EQUITY AND THE TWO-STAGE SELECTION PROCEDURE

We have seen that the school selection process automatically denies many low-achieving students access to Title I services. Even in schools selected for Title I programs, perfect vertical equity does not exist and a substantial proportion of low-achieving students are not chosen to receive Title I services, while those who are less disadvantaged do receive them. In this section we summarize the combined effects of the school-level and student-level selection procedures by estimating the proportion of educationally deprived third and fourth graders in each district who actually receive Title I services. These proportions indicate the extent of coverage of educationally disadvantaged students and may be calculated by multiplying the percentage of all disadvantaged third and fourth graders who attend Title I schools by the percentage of disadvantaged students in these grades who are actually selected to receive Title I services. Table 4-5, presents estimates of coverage for students at each reading level.

The coverage rates for low achievers are generally low. Even for the most seriously disadvantaged—those who are more than one year below grade level in reading—the mean is only 37 percent; the range is 12 to 69 percent.

As is consistent with the intent of Title I, the probabilities of selection decrease as reading levels increase. On a districtwide basis only small percentages of students reading at grade level and above are included in Title I programs, with the exception of Alum Rock and possibly Yonkers. However, these small percentages refer to much larger numbers of students than do percentages of low achievers. Consequently, the coverage rates indicate that Title I is extended to many students who are not low achievers.

These coverage rates for the demonstration districts correspond reasonably well with national estimates made by the Decima Corporation.[15] Decima interviewed parents of some 15,000 public elementary school children in grades one through six. Students determined to be one year or more below grade level on the Comprehensive Tests of Basic Skills were identified as low achievers—consistent with the congressionally mandated definition and roughly consistent with the teachers' rating scale used in the demonstration districts by Abt Associates.

While the average proportion of all low achievers receiving Title I services in the thirteen demonstration districts was 29 percent, the nationwide proportion estimated by Decima was 31 percent. The Decima report also indicated that while 10 percent of the students served by Title I were not low achievers, the estimated *number* of such students (1.3 million) was slightly higher than the number of low-achieving students receiving such instruction (1.2 million). These data suggest that about half of all Title I resources are delivered to children who are not educationally disadvantaged, even though the *percentage* of such students is relatively low. Of course, as noted above, this definition of low achievement is extremely conservative and has been the subject of considerable controversy. Without accepting this particular definition, however, one could still argue that imperfect selection

TABLE 4-5. PERCENTAGES OF STUDENTS IN EACH DISTRICT RECEIVING TITLE I SERVICES, BY READING ACHIEVEMENT LEVEL

			READING ACHIEVEMENT LEVEL		
Districts	More Than 1 Year Below Grade Level	1 Year Below Grade Level	1/2 Year Below Grade Level	At Grade Level	Above Grade Level
Adams County #12	12%	3%	1%	0%	0%
Alum Rock	29	23	29	24	19
Berkeley County	24	8	2	3	26
Boston	52	15	28	11	3
Charlotte	53	35	15	2	4
Harrison County	69	53	26	3	.4
Houston	21	20	12	4	1
Mesa	46	32	21	9	4
Newport	18	23	12	4	.6
Racine	15	13	7	.4	0
Santa Fe	65	41	25	4	2
Winston-Salem	30	28	15	2	0
Yonkers	53	60	46	33	15
Mean	37	27	18	8	5

procedures result in the provision of services to many students who are in less need of such services than their schoolmates.

SUMMARY

At each step in the process of selecting schools and students to participate in the Title I program, district and school practices may refine, extend, and at times confound the intent of federal policymakers. School selection is based on various poverty criteria (used singly or in combination), which are manipulated so as to identify as many eligible schools as possible. Student selection techniques, although based primarily on academic performance, are subject to district-specific tests and cutoff lines and are supplemented by informal decision rules. Thus, while the legal framework is designed to allow districts flexibility in the process of selecting Title I schools and students, the result may not be perfect vertical or horizontal equity.

With respect to school selection different district criteria can lead to different subsets of schools being designated as eligible for Title I. This implies that the automatic exclusion from Title I services of low achievers in non-Title I schools is based on relatively arbitrary standards. Such a situation can result in vertical inequity at the school level.

Student selection within Title I schools also may be inequitable. Generally, a student's chances of being selected for Title I are related to achievement: the lower the level of achievement, the greater the probability of selection. In most of the demonstration districts, however, perfect vertical equity has not been achieved. In addition, factors other than academic achievement seem to play a role in student selection in many districts, suggesting possible horizontal inequities. The ultimate consequence of these school and student selection procedures is that about 69 percent of elementary school low achievers are not served by Title I, whereas many students with less severe academic need are served.

Notes

1. The NIE-sponsored National Survey of Compensatory Education provides data on Title I projects from a nationwide sample of 100 school districts. Survey data refer only to elementary schools. See NIE, *Compensatory Educational Services* (Washington, D.C.: July 31, 1977); and NIE, *Title I Funds Allocation.*

2. The Orshansky poverty index sets poverty-level incomes by estimating the costs of adequate diets for different sizes and types of families, and the typical costs of other goods and services relative to food expenditures.

3. NIE, *Title I Funds Allocation,* p. 60.

4. Ibid., p. 61.

5. Ibid., p. 62.

6. Ibid., p. 63.

7. Ibid.

8. The free lunch data were taken from classroom rosters of all students in sample classrooms. AFDC data were obtained for a subset of these students as well. The poverty results were computed using income and family size data from parent interviews conducted on a still smaller subset of pupils on the rosters.

9. These data are supported by correlations from the national survey. Schools with high numbers of AFDC children are also likely to have high numbers of free lunch recipients (correlation = .81). Other pairs of indicators, however, are less closely related. (The correlation between 1970 census and AFDC is .58; between 1970 census and free lunch, it is .51.) Thus, a district's choice of poverty factors could have important effects on which schools it selects for Title I services. See NIE, *Title I Funds Allocation,* p. 61.

10. Alison Wolf, "The Relationship Between Poverty and Achievement," working note, NIE, December 1977, p. 9.

11. It appears that these teacher ratings are reliable estimates of actual reading achievement. In a validation study conducted in 1976, achievement scores were obtained for a smaller sample of students based on district-administered reading tests and their scores compared to the teachers' ratings. The correlation between the two measures averaged .67 and ranged from .56 to .76.

12. Section 417 (a) (2) of the General Education Provisions Act stated that for the purposes of the Secretary of Health, Education, and Welfare's annual report, the term "educationally disadvantaged" refers to children who are achieving one or more years behind the achievement expected at the appropriate grade level for such children. It should be noted that this definition has recently been superceded, in part based on the findings of the congressionally mandated research studies.

13. When all four variables are entered in the regression equation, the coefficients represent the effects of each student characteristic in predicting Title I status, controlling for the other variables in the equation. The regression coefficients in Table 4-4 indicate the average expected change in the probability of being selected for Title I, given a change of one unit in the independent variables. This probabilistic interpretation is made possible because of the binary nature of the dependent variable, Title I status.

14. In four sites (Adams County #12, Berkeley County, Racine, and Yonkers) Title I status showed a skewed distribution, making regression analysis with a binary dependent variable potentially misleading. Therefore, we duplicated the analysis in these four sites with one using a logit transformation of the dependent variable. In no case did this second analysis affect the basis of our conclusions; coefficient signs, relative sizes of effects, and significance levels remained unaltered. Since a logit transformation does not permit a probabilistic interpretation, we present only the untransformed results here.

15. Vincent J. Breglio, Ronald H. Hinckley, and Richard S. Beal, *Students' Economic and Educational Status and Selection for Compensatory Education* (Washington, D.C.: Decima Research, January 1978).

5

Equity in Student Services

We have seen in chapter four that Title I eligibility and targeting requirements are designed to ensure equity in the selection of children
to receive Title I services. We have also seen that the realities of implementation at the district level have a substantial effect on whether or
not perfect equity is in fact achieved. In this chapter we examine the
issue of equity with respect to the services received by targeted children.

According to the legislation, "Title I funds are to be used to expand and improve the educational programs of [program participants]
and to meet their special, as opposed to ordinary, needs." Chapter
two described six provisions which are designed to ensure that this
occurs. These are the maintenance-of-effort, supplement-not-supplant,
equitably provided (formerly referred to as "ordinarily" provided),
comparability, excess costs, and general aid provisions. Essentially,
these provisions require that school districts not replace regular (or
other compensatory) services with Title I services. The latter are intended to supplement (expand and improve) other services and to
meet special needs over and above those the district ordinarily meets.
The comparability provision, which applies at the school level,
"require[s] that the level of [services provided from state and local

93

funds] in every Title I school should be comparable, i.e., roughly equal, to the average level in non-Title I schools."[1]

As noted in chapter three, there is considerable debate within OE over the means by which these supplemental requirements are to be enforced.[2] Some argue that enforcement should be focused on the use of funds at the district or school level. Others argue that services at the student level must be examined in order to determine compliance. This controversy stems in part from a fundamental conflict over the proper role of the federal government in education and in part from concern about the practical problems associated with gathering within-school data.

Nevertheless, the purpose of the provisions is clear; they are meant to ensure that Title I services expand and supplement the regular educational services offered to Title I children, and that Title I children, as a group, not be deprived of any of the regular or other compensatory services they would ordinarily receive were Title I services not available.

This chapter examines the effects of these regulations on the services received by Title I children. First, we present data from NIE's national survey of 100 school districts to provide a brief overview of the use of Title I funds. Then we use data from the demonstration study to give a more detailed picture of Title I services and to compare the services received by Title I and non-Title I students. Assuming that the services received by non-Title I students represent what is "ordinarily" provided by the district, this comparison allows us to explore the supplementary nature of Title I. Finally, we consider additional data from the demonstration districts and from a large body of research literature in order to explore some of the complexities underlying the issue of equity in services.

USE OF TITLE I FUNDS[3]

According to the national survey data, federal funding for ESEA Title I was approximately $2.4 billion in 1975-76 and accounted for about 3 percent of all federal, state, and local expenditures for elementary and secondary education. These funds were distributed to 13,877 districts, or approximately 90 percent of all U.S. school districts which have elementary school students.

In general, districts concentrated their Title I funds on providing services to public elementary school students. Of the 30 million public elementary school students in 1975-76, 5.9 million (or 19.5 percent) received some form of compensatory services. Approximately 4 percent of all students in private schools also received Title I services.

Despite the concentration of resources at the elementary school level, expenditures per student varied widely across districts; in the thirteen demonstration districts, for example, expenditures ranged from $62 to $727 for each student. This variation is attributable, among other factors, to variation in the amount of funds received by the district per eligible student.

For each eligible student, a district was entitled in 1975-76 to a federal grant worth 40 percent of the state's average per-pupil expenditure (APPE).[4] However, no state's cost factor was permitted to exceed 120 percent of the national APPE, nor could it fall below 80 percent of the national average. Since several categories of children are eligible for Title I, district grants can vary depending upon the numbers of such children. They can also vary depending upon the state's APPE and the manner in which funds are allocated at the subcounty level.

Variation in expenditures also reflects district choices regarding the concentration of resources. Some districts choose to serve a limited number of very low-achieving students, expending a large amount of funds per educationally disadvantaged child. Others prefer to spend less per child in order to distribute Title I funds to a larger number of children. Finally, expenditures per student can vary among the schools within a district. According to national survey data, nearly half the sample districts (45 percent) attempted to distribute Title I funds on the basis of the number of students actually receiving Title I services in particular schools. Other districts distributed their Title I funds in proportion to the number of low-income students in each Title I school. Since students were selected on the basis of educational, not economic, criteria, this means that these school districts did not distribute resources proportionately to students served. The rest of the districts used extremely vague rules for allocating resources, and the level of funding per child varied substantially from school to school. Certain districts, for example, considered one or more of the following factors in deciding how to allocate funds: relating resources to the greatest need; availability of space for pullout instruction, and the desire of principals to participate in the program.

According to the national survey, most Title I funds were used by districts to provide compensatory instruction, as opposed to such noninstructional or auxiliary services as counseling or provision of food and clothing. Approximately 74 percent of Title I funds were spent for instruction, 20 percent for administration, and 5 percent for auxiliary services. Of expenditures for instruction, approximately 53 percent were for reading, 19 percent for math, and 10 percent for language arts. The remaining 18 percent was spent in other instructional areas, such as courses in English as a second language, social/cultural studies, and science.

Approximately 59 percent of all Title I programs provided some types of auxiliary services, but the average portion of Title I expenditures for such services was less than 5 percent. Of the expenditures made for auxiliary services, parent advisory councils accounted for 33 percent, reflecting the importance given to such activities in the federal regulations. Another one-third of auxiliary expenditures typically went for counseling and social work services.

Reflecting the instructional emphasis of most Title I programs, the largest single expenditure item was instructional staff salaries. Although most of these personnel expenditures were made for teacher salaries, it is notable that 54 percent of all teacher aides in Title I districts were supported by Title I funds. Indeed, the availability of Title I funds has had a major impact on the introduction of paraprofessionals into the classroom.

Little comprehensive information about the actual services received by Title I children was available prior to 1975. However, part of NIE's national survey effort focused on providing such information. Survey results revealed that Title I students generally receive instruction in one or two subjects, usually reading or language arts, and that the amount of instruction they receive per week varies by subject area. Children who receive instruction in more than one subject, moreover, tend to receive less instructional time in any one subject. The majority of Title I instruction is provided in a pull out setting, which in most cases means a specially equipped classroom used primarily for compensatory instruction. Title I students typically receive this instruction from instructional specialists or paraprofessional aides in groups consisting of about nine students. The paraprofessional aides, who vary greatly in training and experience, are frequently used to provide students with individual attention.

THE RELATIONSHIP OF TITLE I TO REGULAR SERVICES

Findings from the thirteen demonstration districts generally parallel the national data on Title I services. The demonstration data however, also offer a unique opportunity to compare the services (both compensatory and regular) received by Title I students with those of non-Title I students. This comparison gets at the core of the equity issue in compensatory services.

In describing the relationship between Title I services and services provided with nonfederal (state or local) funds, we focus primarily on language arts instruction in the elementary grades. This is warranted since national data indicate that more than 80 percent of Title I instructional resources are spent in these grades, with approximately 60 percent of that amount spent on language arts instruction. This is also characteristic of expenditures in the demonstration districts.

Demonstration data were gathered directly from teachers of Title I and non-Title I students using an instrument called the Classroom Activities Log (CAL). Designed specifically for the demonstration study, the CAL records data for thirteen subject areas (language arts,[5] mathematics, social studies, and so on). It also provides information on the size of the group in which instruction is delivered and the type of adult involved in its delivery.

In nine of the demonstration districts students in non-Title I schools received more regular language arts instruction than students in Title I schools.[6] The differences range from sixteen minutes favoring Title I to twenty-four minutes favoring non-Title I, and average about seven minutes in favor of students in non-Title I schools. (See Table 5-1).[7]

With respect to student-level differences, Table 5-2 presents the average amount of daily instruction in regular and compensatory language arts received by each of three groups of students: Title I students, non-Title I students in Title I schools, and non-Title I students in non-Title I schools. Title I students were provided with less regular language arts instruction than non-Title I students in the same schools in eleven of the twelve districts. These differences are quite large — averaging eighteen minutes a day. The data in Table 5-2 suggest that the school-level differences depicted in Table 5-1 are attributable to differences between Title I and non-Title I students in the same schools. In fact, the cross-district averages for amount of regular language arts instruction received by the two types of non-Title I students (those in Title I schools and those in non-Title I schools) are the same.[8]

The data portrayed in Table 5-2 indicated that Title I students are provided more compensatory language arts instruction than either type of non-Title I student in each of the districts. Summing regular

TABLE 5-1. AVERAGE MINUTES PER DAY DEVOTED TO REGULAR
CLASSROOM LANGUAGE ARTS BY DISTRICT AND TYPE OF SCHOOL

DISTRICT	TITLE I SCHOOLS*	NON-TITLE I SCHOOLS
Adams County #12	115	119
Alum Rock	86	102
Berkeley County	136	147
Boston	100	106
Charlotte	106	108
Harrison County	131	115
Houston	135	146
Mesa	103	111
Newport	NA	NA
Racine	126	126
Santa Fe	111	106
Winston-Salem	123	138
Yonkers	86	110
Mean	113	120

*Includes both Title I and non-Title I students

Note: Because of small sample sizes, data for Newport were not included in this
analysis.

and compensatory instruction, we see that Title I students also receive more total language arts than their non-Title I counterparts in
all but two districts.

Taken together, these results suggest that Title I students' compensatory language arts instruction replaced a portion of their regular
language arts instruction. This conclusion is also supported by an
analysis of the type of regular classroom instruction reported by classroom teachers to be lost when compensatory services were delivered.
These data indicate that compensatory instruction in language arts
was provided in place of regular language arts instruction an average
of 58 percent of the time. Instruction in mathematics was lost fourteen percent of the time, and instruction in science or social studies
was lost 6 percent of the time. With a fixed-length school day, some
regular instruction has to be lost when compensatory instruction is
delivered. However, it is interesting to note that Title I language arts

TABLE 5-2. AVERAGE MINUTES PER DAY DEVOTED TO REGULAR AND COMPENSATORY LANGUAGE ARTS BY DISTRICT AND TYPE OF STUDENT

DISTRICT	TITLE I STUDENTS			NON-TITLE I STUDENTS IN TITLE I SCHOOLS			NON-TITLE I STUDENTS IN NON-TITLE I SCHOOLS		
	Regular	Compensatory	Total	Regular	Compensatory	Total	Regular	Compensatory	Total
Adams County #12	109	28	137	119	4	123	119	1	120
Alum Rock	69	40	109	94	15	109	102	4	106
Berkeley	111	35	146	141	2	143	147	0	147
Boston	90	42	132	107	3	110	106	2	108
Charlotte	97	35	132	114	2	116	108	1	109
Harrison	120	28	148	139	1	140	115	1	116
Houston	122	38	160	142	6	148	146	3	149
Mesa	96	37	133	106	1	107	111	2	113
Newport*	NA	NA	NA	NA	NA	NA	NA	NA	NA
Racine	112	34	146	134	1	135	126	3	129
Santa Fe	111	27	138	111	0	111	106	2	108
Winston-Salem	112	40	152	133	2	135	138	2	140
Yonkers	69	30	99	98	4	102	110	2	112
Mean	102	35	136	120	3	123	120	2	121

Note: Because of small sample sizes, data for Newport were not included in this analysis.

instruction replaces regular basic skills instruction (reading, mathematics) seventy-two percent of the time, whereas it replaces non-academic services only 20 percent of the time.

Turning now to a comparison of instructional characteristics, we find several notable differences. First, as Table 5-3 shows, Title I students receive compensatory instruction in groups which are much smaller than those characteristic of regular instruction.[9] Regular language arts instruction (for both Title I and non-Title I students) is typically delivered in medium and large groups. In fact, in only one district is more than 50 percent of regular arts instruction delivered to students individually or in small groups. In contrast, in nine districts more than 50 percent of the compensatory instruction is delivered to individuals or small groups.

Second, both the type of instructor providing services and the educational qualifications of the instructor differ. Regular language arts instruction is generally delivered by classroom teachers. In fact, across all districts more than 70 percent of the regular language arts instruction of Title I and non-Title I students is delivered by classroom teachers. In contrast, in ten of the districts less than 10 percent of the compensatory language arts instruction is delivered by classroom teachers. In nine of the districts more than 60 percent of the compensatory instruction is delivered by instructional specialists.

In almost all of the districts specialists appear to be better qualified than classroom teachers in terms of level of education. In nine districts more specialists than classroom teachers had educational training beyond the B.A. In several districts the difference between specialists' and teachers' level of training is striking. With regard to years of teaching experience, specialists in eight of the thirteen districts were slightly less experienced than were classroom teachers. (In only one district were specialists markedly less experienced than classroom teachers; in two they were markedly more experienced.)

Compensatory and regular language arts also differ with regard to the location of instruction. Almost all of the demonstration districts provided Title I language arts in locations other than the regular classroom. In fact, only one district, Alum Rock, did not use the pullout model for compensatory instruction. The outside locations used by the districts were, for the most part, specially equipped resource rooms, laboratories, or learning centers. Regular language arts, on the other hand, was almost always delivered in the regular classroom.

The demonstration study also obtained detailed information on the extent to which various individualized instructional practices

TABLE 5-3. GROUP SIZE FOR REGULAR AND COMPENSATORY LANGUAGE ARTS INSTRUCTION BY STUDENT TYPE (PERCENTAGE OF TIME SPENT IN INSTRUCTIONAL GROUP)*

| | REGULAR LANGUAGE ARTS | | | | | | COMPENSATORY LANGUAGE ARTS | | |
| | TITLE I STUDENTS | | | NON-TITLE I STUDENTS IN TITLE I SCHOOLS | | | NON-TITLE I STUDENTS IN NON-TITLE I SCHOOLS | | |
DISTRICT	Individual	Small	Medium**	Individual	Small	Medium	Individual	Small	Medium
Adams County #12	22%	13%	30%	13%	9%	27%	7%	30%	62%
Alum Rock	42	16	28	16	18	37	36	36	26
Berkeley County	12	19	15	9	5	33	25	46	16
Boston	13	17	46	12	13	47	7	47	44
Charlotte	13	16	39	16	7	35	16	51	34
Harrison County	7	9	34	9	5	28	3	38	59
Houston	7	11	35	7	5	38	6	26	63
Mesa	13	16	19	19	9	19	7	90	3
Newport	NA	NA	NA	NA	NA	NA	NA	NA	NA
Racine	8	4	43	5	2	18	20	80	0
Santa Fe	18	25	39	14	16	35	10	73	16
Winston-Salem	8	7	40	9	6	39	5	50	45
Yonkers	19	13	10	26	8	29	7	61	26

*Percentage of time rather than minutes of instruction is presented to allow cross-district comparisons to be made.
**The percentage of time spent in large group instruction is not included. It may be calculated by summing the percentage of time spent in individual, small, and medium group instruction, and subtracting from 100.

Note: Because of small sample sizes, data for Newport were not included in this analysis.

were used by the demonstration districts for both regular and compensatory language arts. To assess the general level of individualized
instruction within each respondent group, we constructed the Individually Prescribed Activities and Materials Scale.[10] Table 5-4 displays
the mean scores of compensatory language arts specialists and regular
language arts instructors on the scale. The higher the score, the more

TABLE 5-4. MEAN SCORES OF COMPENSATORY LANGUAGE ARTS
SPECIALISTS AND REGULAR LANGUAGE ARTS INSTRUCTORS ON THE
INDIVIDUALLY PRESCRIBED ACTIVITIES AND MATERIALS SCALE*

DISTRICT	COMPENSATORY SPECIALISTS	REGULAR INSTRUCTORS
Adams County #12	61	48
Alum Rock	67	51
Berkeley County	75	42
Boston	60	47
Charlotte	71	51
Harrison County	62	46
Houston	68	48
Mesa	53	48
Newport	NA	NA
Racine	70	45
Santa Fe	59	52
Winston-Salem	73	47
Yonkers	66	56
Mean	65	48

*Scores on this scale were standardized so that a score of 50 represents the mean
of site means for both specialists and regular classroom teachers. The standard
deviation of this scale is .10. Scores derived using this scaling procedure are commonly known as t-scores.

Note: Because of small sample sizes, data for Newport were not included in this
analysis.

frequently teachers utilize individualized teaching methods and materials. In all districts there was a notably higher level of individualization (as measured by the scale) associated with compensatory specialists than with regular teachers.

EQUITY IN SERVICE DELIVERY

As we have seen, Title I and regular services in the demonstration districts differ in several ways. Title I instruction is delivered in smaller classes and by specialists, who generally have a higher level of education than the classroom teachers who provide regular instruction. Furthermore, Title I instruction usually takes place outside of the regular classroom in specially equipped labs or resource rooms, and it is more individualized than regular instruction. In order to receive these compensatory services, Title I children give up some time in regular instruction.

What does this pattern tell us about equity with regard to services? Perhaps most striking is the fact that Title I children do indeed give up some regular instruction in order to receive compensatory language arts. However, districts do not completely replace regular language arts instruction with Title I language arts instruction. As the demonstration data show, losses in regular time are slightly more than offset by gains in compensatory language arts. The net effect is that Title I children receive somewhat more language arts instruction than do non-Title I children. Nevertheless, it is clear that they do not receive as much more as they would if Title I instruction were simply added to regular instruction.

This issue of loss of instructional time is extremely complex. On the one hand, our discussions with local administrators revealed that, from the district perspective, practical considerations militate against simply adding Title I instruction to regular instruction. Perhaps the most fundamental of these is the fact that the length of the school day is usually established by the state and/or local laws that govern education. Also, a structured curriculum leaves few, if any, unfilled moments. Thus, when compensatory instruction is added to a child's instructional program, a regularly scheduled activity must be dropped or reduced.

In deciding which subject or activity to drop or reduce in order to add compensatory instruction, districts are faced with certain legal, pedagogical, and logistical realities. First, state laws usually mandate that specific portions of the school day be devoted to certain subjects (for example, reading, math, science, and physical education). Second, many local school boards and communities are strongly committed to providing additional curriculum components (for example, bilingual education and such enrichment activities as art and music). Third, districts must consider the reactions of both parents and children to the deletion of certain subjects in order to make time for compensatory services. This is particularly important, since children may view Title I as punitive if they are forced to miss what they generally consider to be the more enjoyable aspects of the school day, such as art or music, in order to receive additional instruction in subjects which they find difficult. In addition, parents may object if children completely miss any single area of regular instruction, such as science or social studies, during the school year. Finally, the reactions of teachers to scheduling burdens resulting from the movement of students in and out of their classrooms must be considered.

On the other hand, research evidence from a number of sources points to time for instruction as a critical in-school determinant of student performance.[11] For example, Bloom argues that the learner must be actively involved in instruction, either overtly or covertly, if it is to be effective. He also claims that, considering all the literature on the effects of school, teacher, and student variables on student development, participation is clearly the strongest influence. Furthermore, Bloom asserts that "the slowest 10 percent of students may need about five to six times as much rehearsal, practice, or participation in the learning activity as the most rapid 10 percent of students."[12]

In considering the issue of instructional time, the theoretical distinction between allocated and engaged time is extremely important, particularly for our discussion of equity. Allocated time refers to the amount of time a student is assigned work in a particular area. In contrast, engaged time "is that subset of the allocated time when a student appears to be attending to the learning task."[13] Research results on the relative effects of each have generally been inconclusive; that is, both allocated and engaged time appear to predict student achievement.

Our measures of both regular and compensatory instruction reflect allocated time more than engaged time. As the results described above clearly show, Title I children lose some portion of the time allocated for regular instruction in order to receive compensatory instruction. Do they, however, also lose engaged time? One could argue that the loss of allocated time is actually accompanied by an increase in engaged time. For example, one demonstration district, by mandate of the local school board, maintains an intensive regular reading/ language arts program during the entire morning of each instructional day. It is the policy of the district to schedule Title I instruction during the individual study portion of this program. The argument that administrators make in favor of this decision is that individual study is generally used to reinforce the skills and concepts being taught. Since children who need remedial instruction often have not mastered these skills or concepts, they may not benefit from this portion of the program. By providing intensive remedial instruction (that is, Title I language arts) during this time, the district hopes to achieve greater engaged time than would be achieved during regular instruction, as well as to enhance instruction for Title I students in a number of other ways.[14]

Given that allocated time (as well as engaged time) is also positively associated with achievement gains, one might still be tempted to argue that equity would be better served if Title I children were given their full allocation of regular language arts instruction with Title I instruction simply added. In short, the case might be made that loss in regular instructional time does not expand and improve the educational programs of Title I children, regardless of either the practical considerations militating against such a choice or the possibility that engaged time is actually increased. However, the picture is further complicated by the differences in the nature of Title I and regular services. Given these differences, one might argue that Title I does expand and improve the regular curriculum, regardless of any time lost in regular instruction. Let us consider this position in more detail.

The Nature of Title I Instruction

We must remember that equity demands that Title I instruction not only expand and supplement regular instruction but also be responsive to the special needs of educationally deprived children. As discussed above, districts use a variety of mechanisms in attempting to meet these requirements. Title I children receive "more" in terms of instructor specialization and qualifications, degree of individualization, small class size, and specially equipped resource rooms where instruction takes place.

These features appear to be reasonable ways of providing equity in the sense of expanded and improved special services. For most school districts, these measures are viewed as standard means of ensuring high-quality instruction. In addition, they usually cost more and are therefore likely to satisfy the extra cost requirements of Title I. The research literature, however, raises questions about the actual pedagogical value of some of these mechanisms. Before we can come to any final conclusion about the issues of equity with regard to Title I services, these questions must be explored.

Individualization. Instruction geared toward the individual is more characteristic of compensatory than regular instruction in all of the demonstration districts. According to the conventional wisdom which has emerged over the past decade, individualized instruction is particularly effective in compensatory education programs. Yet the research findings results are inconsistent (which, as several authors have pointed out, may well be the result of the fact that different studies used different definitions of individualized instruction). Early support for the effectiveness of individualization was found in evaluations of successful compensatory programs, particularly those reviewed by Wargo et al. and the Office of Education.[15] While the definitions of individualization reported in these reviews varied to some degree, certain characteristics were common to both, such as clearly written and/or stated academic objectives; attention to individual needs, including individual diagnosis and prescription; and structured sequential instruction. More recent studies of reading and mathematics instruction identify similar elements of individualization as associated with effective instruction.[16]

In contrast to these positive findings, a recent large-scale study found that individualization has variable effects on achievement. The NIE-sponsored Instructional Dimensions Study defined individualization in terms of constructs relating to sequencing and pacing, grouping, and the matching of instruction to student needs. According to this study, there is no clear evidence regarding the superiority of individualized instruction for compensatory education. Although some of the measures designed to reflect various aspects of individualization did show some effect in one or more of the samples studied, there was no consistent pattern across the various subsamples.[17]

Thus, the research evidence on the efficacy of individualization is mixed. As noted above, however, there is considerable variation across the studies in the definition of individualization. (For example, Wargo and OE include group size among the elements of individualization, but other researchers do not.) This variation alone makes it extremely difficult, if not impossible, to state conclusively that individualization does or does not serve the purpose of equity in the sense of expanded and improved services.

Instructor type and qualifications. The research literature offers little to support the compensatory education "specialists" by virtue of their qualifications alone, or improve the nature of Title I instruction over regular instruction. Bloom concludes that the variance in student outcomes accounted for by teacher variables is rarely more than 5 percent.[18] Glass and Smith, while not offering any comment on the relationship between teacher characteristics and pupil achievement, are quite critical of the concept of the compensatory specialist. Citing a study conducted by Coulson et al. in 1977, Glass and Smith note:

> These [inservice training and salary] data seem to indicate that remedial specialists are distinguished neither by their obviously superior [in-service] training nor by the pay they receive for their services. The most cynical assessment of their role and contribution would be that remedial specialist teachers are merely rechristened regular classroom teachers—the motive for so designating them being the need to comply with certain regulations.[19]

We found evidence among the demonstration districts to both support and allay Glass and Smith's concerns. Overall, specialists in the demonstration districts had a higher level of education than did classroom teachers, as noted previously. In a few districts the specialists were also considerably more experienced. In some cases the differences were so marked that the position of specialist appears to have been one of leadership. In other districts, however, where specialists had less experience than classroom teachers and about the same educational level, the designation specialist appears to have been simply a function of the special (Title I) population taught.

From the district perspective, the use of specialists has certain practical advantages. First, the specialist can concentrate on one subject, such as reading. Regardless of educational level or in-service training, this concentration may well have benefits as yet unmeasured by educational research. Moreover, with a normal class load and several subjects to teach, the classroom teacher usually cannot be as responsive as the specialist to the needs of the Title I child.

Class size. The issue of class size has long been debated in educational circles. Although professional organizations have maintained for some time that smaller class size would lead to greater student achievement, researchers have generally been less sanguine. However, in a recent meta-analysis of the class size issue, Glass and Smith report that the relationship between reduced class size and pupil achievement is "clear and strong."[20] According to these researchers, as class

size decreases, achievement increases, particularly as the size goes below twenty pupils. This relationship appears to be slightly stronger in
the secondary grades than in the elementary grades, but it does not
differ appreciably across different school subjects, levels of pupil IQ,
or several other demographic features of classrooms. Thus, it would
appear that the small classes in which Title I students receive compensatory instruction are equitable in the sense of improving regular
instruction and, hence, meeting the special needs of the disadvantaged.

Use of Pullout Instruction. Over and above scheduling decisions,
instructor qualifications, individualization, and class size, districts
also attempt to maintain equitable services by means of pullout instruction. It seems clear that this instructional model has developed
in response to excessively conservative and restrictive interpretations
of the Title I legal framework. As noted in chapter three, these interpretations are made primarily by state educational agencies as a result of OE's failure to develop and disseminate clear guidelines. In
short, the pullout model has not necessarily been selected for ped-
agogic reasons, but rather to comply with state and local perceptions
of federal requirements.

Recent research points to the potentially negative effects of pullout instruction. For example, the Instructional Dimensions Study
showed that pullout instruction was sometimes less effective than
mainstreaming in enhancing student achievement.[21]

In a major examination of research on pullout instruction, Glass
and Smith argue against the pullout model. These authors place great
weight on the data gathered by Coulson et al. in 1977, the results of
which are interpreted by Glass and Smith to indicate "that the greater the proportion of time the pupil spends in 'pull-out' reading or
mathematics, the lower his achievement."[22]

Perhaps even more dramatic evidence of the potentially negative
effects of pullout instruction is provided by a large body of related
research—mainstreaming the handicapped, labeling and teacher expectations, ability grouping, peer tutoring, and desegregation. Although Glass and Smith are careful to qualify the utility of an analogy between these other forms of instruction and pullout, they none-
theless conclude:

> ...in general, research does *not* support the wisdom of instruction
> under conditions...in 'pull out' programs. Pupils pulled out of regular
> classrooms would have to receive remarkably effective compensatory
> programs to offset the potential risks incurred. In our opinion, the 'pulled

out' pupil is placed in moderate jeopardy of being dysfunctionally labeled, of foregoing opportunities for peer tutoring and role modeling, and of being segregated from pupils of different ethnic groups.[23]

Glass and Smith make a powerful argument. Yet its relevance to Title I is somewhat questionable. In Title I programs as they currently operate, pupils are in effect "dysfunctionally labeled" simply by being deemed eligible for Title I services. It is unlikely that pullout instruction per se contributes any more to this problem. Moreover, Title I pupils spend only a small portion of the school day in the lab or resource room. The remainder of the time they are in the regular classroom with their regular classmates and enjoy normal opportunities for "peer tutoring and role modeling," as well as integration. Finally, and perhaps most important, in Title I pullout is associated with increased individualization, somewhat better qualified teachers who specialize in compensatory instruction, and smaller class size. Even if pullout instruction is harmful (which has not been conclusively established), the positive impact of these factors may well offset any harm that it might cause.

SUMMARY AND CONCLUSION

Thus, the issue of equity in delivery of services is extremely complex. In attempting to expand services and supplement regular instruction, districts must first resolve time and scheduling problems associated with a fixed-length school day and various curricular demands. Next, districts must decide how to improve services and meet the special needs of the disadvantaged (for example, through individualized instruction, or reduced class size, or both).

The demonstration districts tried a little of everything as they sought to improve services and meet the special needs of the disadvantaged. Children did lose some regular services as a result of their involvement in Title I instruction, but whether this loss should be viewed as inequitable is not clear. If allocated time is the critical key to school achievement, then the loss of time spent in regular instruction may not be offset by Title I instruction, even if it does provide more engaged time, more individualization, more specialized instructors, smaller group size, and specially equipped classrooms. On the other hand, if the instructional features offered by Title I are the keys to achievement—either singly or in combination—then the loss of time in regular instruction may actually be desirable. Additional research is needed to clarify this critical issue.

Notes

1. NIE, *Administration of Compensatory Education,* p. 9.

2. NIE, *Administration of Compensatory Education.*

3. Unless otherwise noted, descriptions of Title I services in this section are based on the national survey sponsored by NIE and refer to the 1975-76 school year. NIE, *Compensatory Educational Services.* Since few changes were made in the service requirements in the 1978 Amendments to Title I, we would expect this pattern largely to hold true today.

4. Because the appropriations for Title I fall short of the level of authorization, districts do not receive full entitlements of 40 percent.

5. As measured by the CAL instruments, language arts includes listening, library skills, speaking, grammar, reading, creative writing, and penmanship skills; it does not include instruction in English as a second language.

6. Newport, one of the thirteen districts, is not included here and in the remainder of this discussion because of small sample sizes for Title I students.

7. Although not treated in our discussion, a less pronounced but similar pattern was found for mathematics, other academic instruction (defined as science and social studies combined), and nonacademic instruction.

8. Note that non-Title I students in Title I schools also received less regular language arts instruction than those in non-Title I schools in six of the nine districts in which school-level differences were found. However, these differences were quite small compared to the school-level differences, and also compared to the student-level differences (Title I versus non-Title I), and thus do not appear to account for the results.

9. Group size refers to the size of the group in which instruction is delivered. Four categories of group size are discussed: *individual*—instruction is delivered to the student alone; *small*—instruction takes place in a group of two to five students; *medium*—instruction takes place in a group of six to twenty students; and *large*—instruction takes place in groups of more than twenty students, including whole classes.

10. For a more detailed picture of the changes in various individualization practices per se (for example, the use of performance objectives), see D. Catherine Baltzell and Richard Ames, eds., *ESEA Title I Allocation Policy—Demonstration Study: Results of First Year Implementation,* Part II, (Cambridge, Mass.: Abt Associates Inc., April 1979).

11. See, for example, J.H. Block, "The Effects of Various Levels of Performance on Selected Cognitive, Affective and Time Variables," unpublished doctoral dissertation (Chicago: University of Chicago, 1970); L.W. Anderson, "Time and School Learning," unpublished doctoral dissertation (Chicago: University of Chicago, 1973); J.L. David, "Summer Study: A Two-Part Investigation of the Impact of Exposure to Schooling on Achievement Growth, " unpublished doctoral dissertation (Cambridge, Mass.: Harvard University, 1974); D.E. Wiley and A. Harnischfeger, "Explosion of a Myth: Quantity of Schooling and Exposure to Instruction, Major Educational Vehicles," *Educational Researcher* 3 (1974): 7-12; and T.L. Good and T.M. Beckerman, "Time on Task: A Naturalistic Study in Sixth Grade Classrooms," *The Elementary School Journal* 78, no. 3 (1978): 193-201.

12. B.S. Bloom, *Human Characteristics and School Learning* (New York: McGraw-Hill, 1976), p. 122.

13. N.N. Filby, R.S. Marliave, and C.W. Fisher, "Allocated and Engaged Time in Different Content Areas of Second and Fifth Grade Reading and Mathematics Curriculum," paper presented at the annual meeting of the American Educational Research Association, New York, April 1977, p. 3.

14. It should be noted that replacement of regular instruction is not prohibited by either the Title I legal framework or congressional intent. For example, *ESEA Title I Program Guide No. 44*, March 18, 1968 states:

> Probably the most obvious indication of a child's need for special educational assistance under Title I is his inability to respond constructively to the regular school program. In many cases this program can be modified and integrated with the services to be provided under Title I so as to provide the child with a total program adapted to his special needs. In this connection, the requirement that applicants maintain regular school programs in the project areas at the same levels as they would have been maintained if Title I funds were not available applies only to expenditures and not to the program itself. (p. 8)

Furthermore, the House Report on the 1978 Amendments (H.R. 15, May 11, 1978) points out:

> The committee wishes to emphasize that Title I should not be construed to encourage or require any particular instructional strategy. (p. 26)

Finally, in reference to the practice of tracking the educationally disadvantaged into an entirely separate program from regular instruction (which while not encouraged is specifically not prohibited), the committee states:

> To the extent educationally deprived children receive all of their in-
> struction in a separate setting from higher achieving students, the appli-
> cants must be able to show that program participants are receiving
> their fair share of state and local funds and that programs are substantial-
> ly different in quality and content from services offered children in
> regular classrooms and are designed to meet specific needs of children
> to be served. (p. 27)

15. M.J. Wargo et al., "Further Examination of Exemplary Programs for Educa-
ting Disadvantaged Children" (Palo Alto, Calif.: American Institute for Research,
July 1971); M.J. Wargo et al., "ESEA Title I: A Re-analysis".

16. R. Soar, *Follow Through Classroom Process Measurement and Pupil Growth*
(Gainesville, Florida: University of Florida, 1973); J.A. Stallings and D.H. Kasko-
witz, "A Study of Follow Through Implementation," paper presented at the
annual meeting of the American Educational Research Association, San Francisco,
April 1975; and J.E. Brophy and C.M. Everston, "Process-Product Correlations
in the Texas Teacher Effectiveness Study," final report, (Austin: University of
Texas, 1974).

17. Bloom, *Human Characteristics and School Learning*.

18. Bloom, *Human Characteristics and School Learning*.

19. G.V. Glass and N.L. Smith, "'Pull Out' in Compensatory Education"
(Washington, D.C.: Department of Health, Education, and Welfare, 1977), p. 18.
See further T.E. Coulson et al., *The Third Year of Emergency School Aid Act
(ESAA) Implementation* (Santa Monica, Calif.: System Development Corp.,
1977).

20. G.V. Glass and N.L. Smith, "Meta-analysis of Research on Class Size and
Achievement," *Educational Evaluation and Policy Analysis* 1, no. 1 (1979): 2-16.

21. NIE, *Effects of Services on Student Development*.

22. Glass and Smith, "'Pull Out' in Compensatory Education," p. 23.

23. Ibid., p. 41.

PART TWO

How It Might Have Been

= 6 =

Alternative Allocation Options*

A number of theoretical issues confronted—and divided—Congress as it attempted reauthorization of Title I in 1974. Among the more intractable and fraught with emotion was an issue that was basic to the purpose of the program: Was Title I primarily a poverty or an educational program?

Title I was originally conceived as part of the war on poverty in 1965. Yet the legislation has an inherent conflict. While funds are allocated to states, counties, districts, and schools based on poverty criteria, within the schools the services are provided to low-achieving children regardless of family income. Title I services are intended to raise the level of performance of these children to that appropriate for their age. This focus on the educational aspects at the child level has come to be a basic tenet of Title I—as basic as the distribution of money at all other levels based on poverty. Since the services intended to aid the child are paid for with that money, they can only be provided if the money is in the school in the "proper" amounts.

*Adapted from a working note on the NIE compensatory education study: "Alternative Allocation Options," by Ann M. Milne, May 2, 1979.

To phrase the issue as it was often phrased in congressional debates: If three children in a school district have educational need,
why is only one of them receiving Title I services? The child receiving
services attends a Title I-eligible school with a high proportion of *low-
income* children, and the school receives sufficient Title I funds to
serve all of the *educationally* disadvantaged. The second child attends
a Title I school which, because it is in an area with a smaller proportion of low-income families, receives fewer funds—not enough for all
educationally needy children.[1] The third child attends a school that
contains too few low-income children to be eligible for Title I. All
three children are equally in need of compensatory services, but because of poverty-based allocation, two of them cannot receive services.

This apparent inequity became the focus of congressional debate in
1974. The leading proponent of a change to achievement-based allocation was Congressman Albert H. Quie (R.-Minn.), the ranking minority
member of the House Education and Labor Committee. Quie argued
that the economic focus of Title I funds allocation unnecessarily excluded children in need of compensatory instruction. He recognized
the then-current fear that a change to achievement-based allocation
might mean the expansion of the program into middle-class, wealthier
schools, with the possible loss of services in poorer schools. After
all, the funds were limited. However, he argued that expanding the
program into those schools would be likely to draw in a larger, more
politically active and sophisticated constituency, which would in
turn exert pressure on Congress to increase program funding.

The poverty-versus-achievement debate was continued in the
House-Senate conference on the ESEA bill. Congressman Quie could
not be ignored; his support was needed by the majority on other
issues, and there was concern over possible veto of the bill by the Republican President if Quie would not support it. Therefore, a compromise, engineered primarily by Congressman John D. Brademas
(D.-Ind.), was effected in conference committee. Achievement-based
allocation would be tested in the NIE compensatory education study
and reconsidered when Title I came up for reauthorization in 1978.
This compromise was in fact a major impetus for the entire NIE
study.

Quie proposed, and NIE studied, a change to achievement criteria at every step of allocation—to states, to districts, and to schools
within districts. The major concern of this chapter is with the effects

of achievement-based allocation to schools within districts. The effects as higher levels, as determined by NIE, have been reported elsewhere.[2]

The standard regulations which control poverty-based allocation to schools specify only that schools must be below the average district poverty level, thus leaving a number of decisions to the individual district (and/or state). As described in chapter two, the district level of poverty, as well as the school level, can be based on the number poor, the percent poor, or a combination. Poverty can be defined according to several measures (the Orshansky index, AFDC, free lunch eligibility, and so forth), each of which implies a different cutoff, or by a combination of such measures. Once the list of eligible schools is determined, the district can select (target) a lesser number to be served. The higher-ranked schools must be served first, but a school may be skipped if it has a lower incidence of academic need than a lower-ranked school. Once the list of targeted schools is established, the district must determine the actual distribution of funds among the schools; the regulations are least specific at this point.

In suggesting a change in criteria at the district level, the study mandate made no suggestions as to which of these parameters would be subject to change. Would districts still be required to use a district average—average achievement rather than average poverty—to determine eligibility? Would this be an overall average achievement score or percentile, or would it be the average number or percent of children below a specified cutoff? What would be the cutoff? What test would be used? How would targeting of schools and distribution of funds occur? NIE was aware of these questions as it attempted to design the demonstration study, and it was clear that the thrust of the study should be practical. Apart from clarifying the philosophical issues underlying poverty or achievement allocation, Congress was interested in examining the practical consequences of each.

NIE offered interested districts the opportunity to change (1) the current school eligibility formula, using either a new poverty-based formula or one based on educational need; and (2) the extent to which funds were concentrated. Concentration of funds on a limited number of projects and children is in fact required in the Title I regulations, but only to the extent that projects should be of "sufficient size, scope and quality" to assure success. A request for proposals outlining these options was sent to all states and territories. They were asked to solicit proposals from local districts and to submit no more than two to NIE. NIE would then select up to twenty districts—maximum specified in the study mandate—to participate in the demonstration.

NIE in fact selected only sixteen districts, judging that the rest of the proposals were technically unacceptable. The sixteen districts spent the first year of the study (school year 1975-76) refining their proposed allocation strategies. At the end of that year three districts withdrew from the study. NIE thus entered the implementation phase with thirteen school districts, which implemented their new strategies during school years 1976-77 and 1977-78.

DISTRICT ALLOCATION CHANGES

The districts chose an interesting array of allocation strategies. No district proposed a new poverty formula, although two districts continued to use their original formulas (while making other changes), and two districts used poverty criteria in conjunction with achievement criteria. On the other hand, no district selected an exact parallel to the current formula—that is, determining the district average number or percent low-achieving students, and deeming eligible all schools with a higher number or percent.

Seven of the thirteen districts used a direct allocation approach: they simply ignored the school eligibility step, serving all low-achieving students irrespective of the school they attended. These seven districts were: Adams County #12, Colorado; Harrison County, West Virginia; Mesa, Arizona; Newport, Rhode Island; Racine, Wisconsin; Santa Fe, New Mexico; and Alum Rock, California. These districts had served an average of 51 percent of their schools prior to the demonstration; during it they expanded services to include all schools.[3]

Rather than deeming eligible all schools with a number or percent of low achievers above the district average, two districts used a "percent below percentile" method of allocation. They decided that any school having a given percentage of students below a certain test percentile, using national norms, would be eligible. This option was based upon the assumption that, given normal test score distributions, a school with X percent of students below the Xth percentile could be considered average. However, a school with more than X percent of students below the Xth percentile could be considered to have a concentration of students in need of special services. The two districts choosing this option were Charlotte, North Carolina (which selected all elementary schools in which 35 percent or more of the students were below the 30th percentile), and Winston-Salem, North Carolina (which selected all elementary schools in which 40 percent or more of the students were below the 35th percentile). In both districts, this procedure led to an increased number of Title I schools. Charlotte had served 67 percent of its elementary schools prior to the demonstration; it served 76 percent during the first year of the demonstration. In Winston-Salem the change was from 35 to 65 percent during the first year.

Two districts elected to use a combination of poverty and achievement measures to determine school eligibility. In Boston, Massachusetts, all schools eligible by poverty were served; schools above the poverty cutoff were reranked by three different achievement measures, and nine were selected for Title I services. In Houston, Texas, all schools were ranked by achievement (percent of students below the 18th percentile). All schools which had previously been served on the basis of poverty eligibility continued to receive services; nine new schools were served based on the achievement rankings.

Finally, two school districts continued to base school eligibility on poverty measures but made major changes in the number and types of students served. These districts were Berkeley County, West Virginia, and Yonkers, New York.

Whether by deliberate choice or simply as a by-product of changes in school selection procedures, all the districts selected more schools during the demonstration than they had before it (see Table 6-1). The increase is most marked in the direct allocation districts. None of the districts were to receive increased Title I funding by virtue of their participation in the demonstration. Would they be forced to decrease the number of students served within the Title I schools in order to maintain per-pupil expenditures, or would they decrease such expenditures and thereby serve more students?

Generally, the districts served more students during the demonstration than they had prior to it (see Table 6-2). However, the proportional increase in number of students served was slightly less than the proportional increase in number of schools, and eight districts did in fact serve fewer students per school. Two others served approximately the same number of students per school during the demonstration as they had previously. Three districts made deliberate attempts to serve more children per school. These three districts (with one other) saw the demonstration as a chance to experiment with new student eligibility procedures.

Berkeley County, West Virginia, attempted to serve more students in a given school by (1) increasing the number of students in each Title I classroom, and (2) using new criterion-referenced tests, keyed

TABLE 6-1. CHANGE IN NUMBER OF ELEMENTARY SCHOOLS SERVED BY TITLE I IN DEMONSTRATION DISTRICTS

	1975-76			1976-77			1977-78		
	NO. OF SCHOOLS	NO. SERVED	% SERVED	NO. OF SCHOOLS	NO. SERVED	% SERVED	NO. OF SCHOOLS	NO. SERVED	% SERVED
DIRECT ALLOCATION DISTRICTS									
Adams County #12	16	3	19%	16	16	100%	16	16	100%
Harrison County	30	25	83	30	30	100	28	28	100
Mesa	25	14	56	25	25	100	26	26	100
Newport	9	3	33	9	9	100	9	9	100
Racine	33	16	48	33	33	100	33	33	100
Sante Fe	16	11	69	16	16	100	16	16	100
ACHIEVEMENT ALLOCATION DISTRICTS									
Charlotte	73	49	67	75	57	76	75	37	49
Winston-Salem	37	13	35	37	24	65	37	23	62
OTHER DISTRICTS									
Alum Rock	19	9	47	18	18	100	18	18	100
Berkeley County	13	10	77	14	11	79	14	11	79
Boston	117	65	56	108	74	69	103	71	69
Houston	169	54	32	169	58	34	167	57	34
Yonkers	31	9	29	25	9	36	25	10	40

TABLE 6-2. CHANGE IN NUMBER OF ELEMENTARY SCHOOL STUDENTS
SERVED BY TITLE I IN DEMONSTRATION DISTRICTS

	1975-76	1976-77	1977-78
DIRECT ALLOCATION DISTRICTS			
Adams County #12	174	591	582
Harrison County	1,409	1,823	1,766
Mesa	2,494	3,229	3,787
Newport	175	445	430
Racine	760	1,552	1,472
Sante Fe	735	1,149	1,205
ACHIEVEMENT ALLOCATION DISTRICTS			
Charlotte	6,440	5,924	6,038
Winston-Salem	1,812	3,310	3,309
OTHER DISTRICTS			
Alum Rock	3,962	9,560	9,217
Berkeley County	630	1,106	1,059
Boston	10,130	10,572	9,538
Houston	19,518	17,854	20,568
Yonkers	2,375	2,855	3,006

to new teaching curricula. If children could be brought up to a particular performance level in less than a full year's time, school administrators believed they could open up classroom space for other students in need.

Alum Rock, California, identified half of its schools as "saturated" and served all students in these schools, rather than only low achievers. This approach appealed to the district for two reasons: (1) it had a large number of low achievers in the system (85 percent of children scored below the 50th percentile on district-administered tests) and (2) since it delivered Title I services in the regular classroom, rather than pulling students out to attend special classes, it could administer services to all children in a classroom efficiently.

Yonkers, New York, attempted to remove the stigma associated with remedial services by serving whole classrooms or large segments of classrooms in Title I laboratories. The services received there by each child were tailored to individual needs—from intensive services to students with severe problems to independent work by those students needing the least help.

A fourth district experimented with a novel student selection process which did not increase the numbers of students served per school. Newport, Rhode Island, assigned a weighted score to each student, based in part on the measured gap between the student's potential and his or her actual achievement.

The remainder of the districts generally did not change student selection criteria drastically. In some cases student selection procedures were tightened; in other cases test cutoffs were changed. It may be noted here that the actual cutoffs established administratively may have little to do with the achievement levels of children actually served. Title I regulations require that students with the greatest academic need be given priority. A district may state that all students performing below the 35th percentile are eligible for services, but it may only have sufficient funds to serve students up to the 18th percentile. An interesting attempt to circumvent this problem was made by Mesa, Arizona. Mesa established priority service areas (intensive help in reading in the first three grades, math in the next three); determined the number of children that could be served with existing resources; and then established, grade by grade for each subject, the cutoff that would produce that number of students. Thus, student eligibility and targeting were accomplished in a single step.

Finally, a number of districts made one further type of allocation change which is worth mentioning. Under standard regulations, once a district has determined which schools are eligible and which are to be targeted, there are few rules specifying the precise amount of funds/services which should be provided to each school. It is generally specified that the "most disadvantaged" schools should receive the greatest support. Although OE Program Guide 44 specified that most disadvantaged would refer to schools with the greatest concentration of low-income children, that guide is now obsolete. Moreover, given the inherent tension between poverty- and achievement-based allocation in Title I, which operates precisely at the point where the monies are translated into services within schools, a good case could have been made for providing the most funds/services to those schools with the greatest number of low achievers.

Prior to the demonstration the thirteen districts solved this dilemma in various ways. One district allocated equal funds to each of the targeted schools, regardless of the concentration of low-income or low-achieving students, feeling this approach was most "fair." Another district, following state requirements, distributed funds to schools in proportion to the concentration of low-income students. State policy was based on the assumption that schools with high concentrations of low-income students, regardless of actual number, have particular problems. In practice, this requirement resulted in schools with the highest poverty ranking being flooded with more services than they could comfortably house or deliver. Still other districts made a rough match between amount of funds and *number* of low-achieving students, believing that the funds should be proportionally available for targeted students in each of the served schools.

In the spring of 1976, when the demonstration districts submitted their final implementation plans to NIE, many of the demonstration districts presented a distribution scheme based on number of low achievers per school, even if they had previously used other schemes. Apparently, for some these changes resulted from having to justify their proposed allocation procedures to NIE. Those two or three districts which did not offer such a scheme were "encouraged" to do so by NIE, in an attempt to stabilize at least one of the multiple processes undergoing change. It is not clear to what extent this encouragement affected the study. Probably the major effect was to sensitize the NIE staff, and later the drafters of the 1978 ESEA bill, to the need for clarifying statutes and regulations in this area. In fact, the 1978 amendments include a new section requiring that funds be allocated among schools on the basis of the number and needs of educationally disadvantaged children [Sec. 124 (e)].

REASONS FOR CHANGING ALLOCATION

The districts' reasons for desiring to participate in the demonstration, as well as the particular changes they wished to make, were outlined in their initial proposals to NIE. Some districts changed the particulars during the planning year, as they attempted to predict the likely consequences of their choices. The six rationales repeatedly expressed in the districts' initial plans (in order of frequency) were:

1. the desire to serve both schools and students on the basis of educational disadvantage;

2. the desire to continue service to Title I-type students relocated by desegregation;

3. the desire to eliminate the distributional inequities caused
by lack of reliability and/or validity of available poverty
indices;

4. the desire to eliminate the stigma of Title I as a special
racial or income group program;

5. the desire to use a "more reasonable" achievement criterion than poverty; and

6. the desire to increase the efficiency of institutional delivery of services.

The first two concerns were each expressed by six districts, two
of which offered both rationales. It is interesting to note that ten of
the thirteen districts offered one or both of these rationales for
participation.

The first concern was best expressed by Santa Fe, which pointed
out that educational deprivation "does not respect" family income,
family residence, or school attendance boundaries. Thus, identifying
children as eligible to receive Title I services on the basis of "accidents
of residence and/or income" is not adequately responsive to educational needs. This argument implies a desire to change two aspects of
current regulations: use of poverty to determine school eligibility,
and concentration of services in a limited number of schools.

The second rationale was offered by five of the six districts that
have desegregated since 1970 (Racine, Charlotte, Winston-Salem,
Boston, and Houston). The sixth, Newport, did not express this concern in its proposal, but stated it during the planning year. This
"follow-the-child" problem arises as children who have been receiving
Title I services are relocated to schools with lower poverty ranking
and can no longer receive services because their schools are not eligible
for Title I. The problem could have been solved without a basic
change in allocation criteria if follow-the-child services had been allowed by Title I.

Four districts criticized poverty indices (the third concern). Berkeley County reported "major discrepancies" between AFDC survey
data and actual population patterns, and cited serious problems with
locating, by school, AFDC children whose surname differed from
that of their parents. Boston pointed out that, because of the high
cost of living in the area, nationally accepted definitions of poverty

were discriminatory. Mesa, a district dominated by the religious and moral tenets of a large Mormon population, noted that many families who qualified for AFDC and/or free lunch assistance did not apply for this help. Mesa also pointed out that 1970 census data were outmoded. Finally, Winston-Salem emphasized that poverty measures were unreliable, tending to become outdated as public assistance rolls fluctuated and populations shifted with urban development.

Concern about stigma prompted five districts to change their allocation procedures. Some argued that a change in selection criteria that permitted more schools to be served would increase the visibility of the Title I program and thereby promote community acceptance and support. Newport noted that, because it made use of poverty criteria, Title I was seen as a poverty program, thus incurring a social stigma displeasing to both parents and school administrators. Charlotte, a conservative southern district which underwent (and resisted) court-ordered desegregation in 1971, explained that federal programs in general, and Title I particularly, were seen as being primarily "for blacks." If poverty criteria were removed, Title I services might be more evenly distributed across all ethnic groups.

The fifth rationale was used by three districts. Both Houston and Winston-Salem argued that achievement criteria are more effective than poverty criteria in determining educational need. Winston-Salem also stated that the criterion for school selection should be the same as that for student selection (that is, achievement). Mesa was concerned with accountability and pointed out that achievement measures can be used not only to determine school eligibility, but also to monitor and evaluate progress.

The sixth rationale was used by three districts. As noted earlier, Berkeley County and Yonkers wished to serve many more children, and they generally succeeded. Santa Fe had initially hoped to increase the number of students served, but parents in the original Title I schools, fearing a dilution of services in their schools, held student expansion to a minimum.

DISTRICT EXPERIENCE WITH ALLOCATION CHANGES

The districts most satisfied with their new allocation procedures were those which made the most dramatic changes in schools served—the direct allocation districts. In fact, as the demonstration drew to a close, these districts were the most vociferous in their desire to continue using the new allocation procedures; a write-in campaign aimed at Congress was encouraged by one of the direct allocation districts. Most districts wanted at least one additional year of waived allocation regulations in order to work back gradually into the old allocation methods if congressional action made this necessary. NIE had consistently made clear to the districts that waivers could not be extended beyond 1977-78, the last year of the study. However, as that year approached, and the ESEA bill was still working its way through Congress, amendments were offered in each house to allow the thirteen districts to continue their new procedures through 1978-79. Encouraged, two of the direct allocation districts decided to risk maintaining the allocation changes. When the smoke cleared in October, 1978, the new ESEA bill did not contain protective provisions for the districts. In August of 1979 Congress passed a retroactive technical amendment (effective October 1, 1978) allowing the demonstration districts to proceed in school year 1978-79 as they had in the preceding year. This amendment protects these two districts against later audit exceptions. The report accompanying the amendments noted that this was done to "help these districts, whose demonstrations were quite useful in determining amendments to Title I last year, make a smooth transition to the new Title I legislation."

It is not difficult to see why direct allocation should be so popular. Providing some services to all schools in the district eliminates the pressure on administrators from school staff and parents who have not traditionally received these services. Moreover, it eliminates the common occurrence of schools being eligible in one year but not in the next, with the consequent loss of services.[4] Finally, an unintended consequence of the direct allocation method was to exempt the districts using it from the obligation to file comparability reports—a task disliked by most districts because of the paperwork involved, even if they support the philosophy of comparability. Since comparability is computed by comparing each Title I school to the average of all non-Title I schools, and there were no non-Title I schools in the direct allocation districts during the demonstration, comparability could not be computed in those districts.

Despite the popularity of the direct allocation method, it must be noted that only small or medium-sized districts used it. Neither Boston nor Houston, the two largest districts, seriously contemplated such a change. Despite the fact that the percentage change in schools served would be no greater in a large district (about twice as many), increasing the absolute numbers of schools by so many is probably administratively and fiscally beyond the capabilities of large districts. Moreover, it is not clear that even the smaller districts could support this expansion indefinitely, at least not without drastically reducing the number of students served within each school.

The two districts that elected to substitute achievement ranking for poverty ranking both encountered difficulties related directly or indirectly to the method selected. Winston-Salem discovered the non-compatibility of standardized achievement tests when they switched from one to another the second year of the demonstration. They found that only three schools would be eligible using the new achievement test (with the same criterion), whereas twenty-four schools had qualified using the first test the year before. Rather than change the criterion or serve only three schools, Winston-Salem elected to "hold harmless" during the second year all the achievement-eligible schools served in the first year.

Charlotte's problems were apparently more directly related to the chosen allocation method and criterion. While retaining the same standardized achievement test both years, the district nevertheless lost eligible schools from one year to the next. In 1976-77 fifty-seven schools were eligible using the achievement measure; in 1977-78 that number dropped to thirty-seven. Had Charlotte been able to continue the new procedures in 1978-79, only eighteen schools would have been eligible. Although it is not clear why the number of achievement-eligible schools decreased, it is possible that the district's criterion—whereby a school qualified if thirty-five percent of the students were performing below the 30th percentile—was to blame. Using such a criterion, even a slight improvement in scores could presumably make the school ineligible.

Out of concern for the purity of the experiment, Charlotte decided to serve only the decreased number of schools deemed eligible each year rather than changing the criterion or holding harmless schools which had previously qualified. However, at the end of the demonstration district administrators expressed dissatisfaction with their choice; if they had to do it again, they avowed, they would choose direct allocation.

Those districts that elected either to combine poverty with achievement criteria or to use poverty alone naturally had little difficulty in returning to predemonstration status. As noted earlier, this group included the two largest districts in the study, both of which served a core group of poverty-eligible schools with a few schools added on the basis of an achievement criterion.

OTHER POSSIBILITIES FOR ALLOCATION

It is interesting to speculate on the effects of other allocation methods not chosen by the districts, such as new poverty criteria, other achievement-based criteria, or a combination of the two. New poverty criteria, or at least new measures or weightings of the standard poverty indicators (family income and AFDC) have been discussed by Congress in relation to the interdistrict allocation of funds since the beginning of Title I. In fact the various weights used in the federal allocation formula have been changed from time to time, most notably the contribution of AFDC. Also, the original flat figure used to define poverty was abandoned in favor of the Orshansky index, which takes family size into account and adjusts somewhat for the cost of living. In other research conducted as part of its overall study, NIE simulated the effects of alternative poverty formulas on interdistrict allocation. The effects were predictable and have been generally known to Congress for some time—for example, the fact that the inclusion of larger proportions of AFDC recipients in the formula works to the advantage of states with well-developed AFDC programs and large urban areas.

Alternative poverty criteria for intradistrict allocation are less well-known and were apparently of little interest to the districts applying for the demonstration study. Whether as a result of this lack of interest or for other reasons, Congress in 1978 also showed little interest in tinkering with intradistrict poverty formulas beyond the expressed concern that the measures of poverty be consistent across all schools within a district.

Achievement-based allocation procedures other than those selected by the demonstration districts received more attention. NIE and Abt Associates were particularly concerned about the lack of an exact parallel to standard poverty-based allocation—that is, deeming eligible all schools below the district's average achievement level. We therefore collected school-by-school poverty and achievement data for each district (district-specified) and simulated the effects on the numbers and types of schools and students that would have been selected. Details of these results are described in chapter seven. Generally, achievement-based alternatives that parallel the current procedure produce larger available pools of low achievers than do poverty-based criteria. However, the advantage is due almost entirely to the ability of achievement-based school eligibility procedures to select more schools than are selected under poverty. This in turn is due to the different distributions of poverty and achievement across a district's schools.

However, because these results are simulated rather than demonstrated, they give us only limited information about actual consequences. For example, we have no practical analogue of the Charlotte experience using a below-district-average criterion, and thus we have no way of knowing whether the numbers of schools deemed eligible would diminish over time—or what a district would choose to do about it.

The 1978 Amendments contain a provision which permits, but does not require, dual ranking of schools using poverty and achievement for purposes of determining eligibility [Sec. 122(a)(2)(A)]. It is not easy to predict the probable consequences of such an approach. The demonstration study collected sufficient data on both poverty and achievement measures at the school level to determine that both change over time in not entirely parallel, predictable, or consistent ways. School eligibility based on a combined poverty-achievement allocation procedure might in the long run be less stable than either type of measure used alone.

Notes

1. While half of the Title I districts actually distribute funds among Title I schools based on the number of low achievers rather than on the number or percent of poor families, it is not a practice specifically mandated by either the statute or the regulations.

2. See, for example, NIE, *Using Achievement Scores to Allocate Title I Funds* (Washington, D.C.: NIE, September 30, 1977).

3. With two exceptions, these districts limited the Title I program to all elementary schools rather than all schools.

4. It should be noted that service continuity within schools is protected to some extent by regulations allowing an ineligible school to be served if it was eligible and served in either of the two previous years.

7

Effects of Alternative Allocation on the Students Served: Demonstrations and Simulations

The demonstration study was initiated in response to congressional interest in new allocation procedures for Title I resources. As discussed in chapter six, Congressman Albert H. Quie, in particular, felt that existing school and student selection procedures did not provide an efficient means of delivering services to those most in need of them—that is, the educationally disadvantaged students whose reading and mathematics performance was far below grade level. The evidence presented in chapter four by and large supports Congressman Quie's contention: many low achievers are excluded from Title I services because of where they live and, to some extent, because of the selection procedures used within schools. Conversely, many students who are not low achievers are included in Title I programs.

The results of the allocation changes made by the demonstration districts provide insight into some of the central questions in the debate over the Title I program. In broad terms they enable us to see what happens when school districts have greater discretion in allocating Title I resources. More specifically they highlight the key selection issues raised in chapter four: maximizing equity in the selection process and maximizing coverage for educationally disadvantaged students.

Interpretations of demonstration results are inevitably limited, because factors apart from the treatment variable of interest cannot be held constant. It is often difficult to determine the extent to which a given outcome is the result of the specific intervention or of other factors associated with it. Therefore, in addition to examining school and student outcomes in the demonstration sites, this chapter presents the results of simulated allocation procedures in which other variables are held constant.

CHANGES IN DISTRIBUTIVE EQUITY

In chapter four we defined vertical equity as the focusing of Title I services on educationally disadvantaged students, beginning wih those whose needs are greatest and proceeding through diminishing degrees of need until resources are exhausted. We also saw that there was a certain amount of vertical inequity in the programs as they existed prior to the demonstration. At this point, it is appropriate to ask whether the demonstration resulted in increased equity and, if so, to what extent.

A rough measure of vertical equity is the proportion of Title I students in a district whose reading level is a year or more below grade level. As noted in chapter four, however, this is a stringent definition of low achievement; the actual definition varies among districts. Technically, some vertical inequity could exist even if all Title I students were low achievers.[1] This would occur if some of the neediest low-achieving students were denied services, while less needy low achievers received them. Hence, using proportion of Title I students who are low achievers as a measure of vertical equity could produce an underestimate of vertical inequity. However, as a practical matter, if we found that all Title I funds went to low achievers, we could conclude that substantial vertical equity existed.

Table 7-1 shows these proportions for the year prior to the demonstration (the baseline year) and the first year of the demonstration. The mean change was only 4 percent, the range from –12 to 18. Five districts showed statistically significant increases, two showed statistically significant decreases, and the rest remained unchanged, at least insofar as our measures can tell. Overall then, there was only a slight tendency for districts to sharpen their targeting on educationally disadvantaged students, and no one allocation method seems to be better than the others in targeting resources on these students.[2]

TABLE 7-1. PERCENTAGE OF TITLE I STUDENTS IN DEMONSTRATION
DISTRICTS WHO ARE LOW ACHIEVERS*

| | PERCENTAGE OF STUDENTS | | CHANGE IN PERCENTAGE |
	Baseline Year	Year One	Year One-Baseline Year
DIRECT ALLOCATION DISTRICTS			
Adams County #12	83	74	-9
Harrison County	67	68	1
Mesa	44	62	18**
Newport	53	66	13
Racine	60	58	-2
Santa Fe	64	72	8**
ACHIEVEMENT ALLOCATION DISTRICTS			
Charlotte	83	79	-4***
Winston-Salem	72	88	16*
OTHER DISTRICTS			
Alum Rock	49	54	5**
Berkeley County	79	67	-12***
Boston	65	64	-1
Houston	67	67	0
Yonkers	61	72	11**
Mean	65	69	4

*Low-achieving students are defined as those reading one year or more below grade level.
**Significant at p ≤ .05
***Significant at p ≤ .05 but accompanied by change in the non-Title I group.

While vertical equity was not much improved as a result of the demonstration, coverage of low-achieving students was increased. As Table 7-2 shows, with only two exceptions (Houston and Yonkers)

TABLE 7-2. PERCENTAGE OF LOW-ACHIEVING STUDENTS IN DEMONSTRATION DISTRICTS COVERED BY TITLE I*

	PERCENTAGE OF STUDENTS		CHANGE IN PERCENTAGE
	Baseline Year	Year One	Year One-Baseline Year
DIRECT ALLOCATION DISTRICTS			
Adams County #12	7%	29%	22%
Harrison County	59	75	16
Mesa	38	47	9
Newport	20	44	24
Racine	14	44	30
Santa Fe	51	66	15
ACHIEVEMENT ALLOCATION DISTRICTS			
Charlotte	44	54	10
Winston-Salem	26	38	12
OTHER DISTRICTS			
Alum Rock	27	99	72
Berkeley County	26	45	19
Boston	47	59	12
Houston	21	20	-1
Yonkers	54	47	-7
Median	38	51	18

*Low-achieving students are defined as those reading one year or more below grade level.

larger proportions of low achievers received Title I services during the first year of the demonstration than before, a mean increase of 8 percent. It would be surprising if this were not the case, because, as we have seen, most districts served more Title I students during that year.

As a group the direct allocation districts showed the strongest and most consistent increases in the coverage of educationally disadvantaged students, with Adams County #12, Newport, and Racine registering large gains. Alum Rock also showed a large increase in coverage, from 27 to 99 percent. This was a direct result of its decision to extend Title I services to all schools and to all eligible students in a subset of these schools.

Comparing proportional increases in Title I schools, Title I students, and coverage of low achievers during the demonstration (see Table 7-3), we see a rough correspondence in the three sets of figures. The districts that show large increases in one set of figures tend to show large increases in the others, the smaller increases also running true to form. In terms of means, the districts increased the coverage of disadvantaged students, more than they increased the number of Title I students, but a closer examination of the figures reveals that this is not really the case. In five districts—Adams County #12, Racine, Charlotte, Boston, and Alum Rock—the increase in coverage was greater than the increase in the number of Title I students. In four districts—Newport, Santa Fe, Winston-Salem, and Yonkers—the increase in coverage was smaller than the increase in numbers of Title I students (or the decrease was greater); and in the remaining four districts—Harrison County, Mesa, Houston, and Berkeley County—the differences were only 5 percent or less.

By and large then, it seems that the districts expanded their Title I programs without sharpening their focus on the educationally disadvantaged. Although there were significant variations in the pattern, districts tended to add new low achievers and other students to the program in about the same ratio as in the past.

SIMULATED ALLOCATION PROCEDURES

While the demonstration provided a great deal of information about the practical consequences of using different allocation procedures, the fact that so many other things changed during the demonstration made it difficult to isolate the effects of the allocation procedures themselves. Moreover, some allocation methods of interest in the debate over Title I were not tried in the demonstration. For these reasons among others, we conducted a number of simulations to "try out" different methods while holding all other factors constant.

Direct Allocation with Perfect Targeting

As previously noted, the demonstration districts increased their coverage of the educationally disadvantaged; however, they did so inef-

TABLE 7-3. PERCENTAGE CHANGE IN NUMBER OF SCHOOLS AND
STUDENTS RECEIVING TITLE I SERVICES AND IN COVERAGE OF
EDUCATIONALLY DISADVANTAGED FROM
BASELINE YEAR TO YEAR ONE*

	CHANGE IN NUMBER OF SCHOOLS	CHANGE IN NUMBER OF STUDENTS	CHANGE IN COVERAGE
DIRECT ALLOCATION DISTRICTS			
Adams County #12	433%	240%	314%
Harrison County	20	29	28
Mesa	79	29	24
Newport	200	154	114
Racine	106	104	214
Santa Fe	45	56	29
ACHIEVEMENT ALLOCATION DISTRICTS			
Charlotte	16	-8	22
Winston-Salem	85	83	41
OTHER DISTRICTS			
Alum Rock	100	141	267
Berkeley County	10	76	73
Boston	14	4	25
Houston	7	-9	-5
Yonkers	0	20	-13
Mean	86	71	87

$$*\text{Percentage change} = \frac{\text{year one} - \text{baseline year}}{\text{baseline year}}$$

ficiently. They served more students—both advantaged and disadvantaged—but, as we shall see in chapter eight, they spent more money
doing it. This raises the question of how well the districts could have

done not only by expanding services to all schools, but also by allocating their initial resources more efficiently. We can simulate coverage in a perfectly efficient direct allocation system by dividing the number of Title I students served in the baseline year in a district by the number of low-achieving students in that district.

Table 7-4 shows the percentages of educationally disadvantaged students served during the baseline year and the first year of the demonstration and under simulated direct allocation with perfect targeting. Overall, the simulated approach would result in coverage as good as or slightly better than that achieved by the demonstration districts. The average coverage for the simulation is 58 percent, for the demonstration it is 52 percent. In six districts—Harrison County, Mesa, Santa Fe, Alum Rock, Boston, and Yonkers—the simulation would result in more coverage; in five districts—Adams County #12, Newport, Racine, Berkeley County, and Houston—it would result in less. In two districts—Charlotte and Winston-Salem—there would be no substantial difference. Even in the six districts where direct allocation was actually tried and increased coverage was most dramatic, the demonstration did not produce markedly better results than could be achieved by perfect targeting within existing resource constraints. In three of these six the demonstration would yield greater coverage and in the other three, less.

Perfect Targeting Within Schools

Even within existing Title I schools perfect targeting could substantially increase the proportion of low achievers served. This can be seen by comparing student selection rates in the baseline year with the results of a simulated student selection process which is perfectly efficient. The simulated selection rate is the ratio of the total number of students served in Title I schools to the number of low achievers in those schools during the year prior to participation in the demonstration. A rate under 100 indicates that even with perfect targeting not all low-achieving students could be served. A rate of 100 percent shows that the district could serve all low-achieving students in Title I schools, but has not done so. A comparison of the actual and simulated selection rates for low achievers in Title I schools is presented in Table 7-5.

The comparison is striking: in six of the thirteen districts *all* disadvantaged students in Title I schools could have been served if the selection process had been perfectly accurate. Moreover, in four

TABLE 7-4. PERCENTAGE OF LOW-ACHIEVING STUDENTS RECEIVING
TITLE I SERVICES IN BASELINE YEARS AND YEAR ONE AND
UNDER THE DIRECT ALLOCATION SIMULATION*

	BASELINE YEAR	YEAR ONE	DIRECT ALLOCATION SIMULATION
DIRECT ALLOCATION DISTRICTS			
Adams County #12	7%	29%	8%
Harrison County	58	74	85
Mesa	38	47	84
Newport	21	45	39
Racine	14	44	25
Santa Fe	51	66	78
ACHIEVEMENT ALLOCATION DISTRICTS			
Charlotte	45	55	54
Winston-Salem	29	41	40
OTHER DISTRICTS			
Alum Rock	27	45	54
Berkeley County	26	60	33
Boston	48	19	74
Houston	20	99	30
Yonkers	53	46	87
Mean	34	52	53

*Low-achieving students are defined as those reading one year or more below
grade level.

other districts resources were sufficient to provide services to 80 percent or more of the low-achieving students in these schools. In two
districts—Alum Rock and Newport—the proportion of low-achieving
students served by Title I programs could almost have been doubled
by achieving complete vertical equity in the distribution of resources.

TABLE 7-5. PERCENTAGE OF LOW-ACHIEVING STUDENTS SERVED IN SCHOOLS DURING THE BASELINE YEAR: ACTUAL AND SIMULATED PROPORTIONS*

	ACTUAL RATE	SIMULATED RATE	DIFFERENCE IN PERCENTAGE
DIRECT ALLOCATION DISTRICTS			
Adams County #12	30%	36%	6%
Harrison County	72	100	28
Mesa	65	100	35
Newport	46	85	39
Racine	38	67	29
Santa Fe	65	98	33
ACHIEVEMENT ALLOCATION DISTRICTS			
Charlotte	66	80	14
Winston-Salem	77	100	23
OTHER DISTRICTS			
Alum Rock	52	100	48
Berkeley County	36	44	8
Boston	71	100	29
Houston	56	86	30
Yonkers	86	100	14
Mean	58	84	26

*Low-achieving students are defined as those reading one year or more below grade level.

Achievement-Based Allocation

Direct allocation was the most commonly proposed alternative to the existing two-stage process of selecting schools on the basis of poverty and selecting students within those schools on the basis of educational disadvantage. Charlotte and Winston-Salem chose another alternative: allocation based on achievement. However, neither district adopted the most straightforward method of achievement allocation, which would be to parallel existing regulations by substituting achievement for the poverty criterion. Using this approach, all schools having percentages (or numbers) of low-achieving students greater than the districtwide proportion (or number) would be eligible for Title I services. Would there be advantages to adopting this procedure in preference to the existing poverty-based method? How many schools and low-achieving students would be eligible for Title I under each?

Table 7-6 shows the simulated effects of poverty and achievement-based school selection procedures (percentage method) on the proportion of schools and low-achieving students eligible for Title I services. (Data were available for only eleven districts.) A look at the mean percentages suggests that a larger proportion of schools and low-achieving students would be eligible for Title I under the achievement-based selection procedure.[3]

A closer examination of the data largely confirms this impression. The proportion of elementary schools eligible for Title I would be greater in nine of the eleven districts if the achievement-based method were used. In one district—Harrison County—there would be no change; and in another—Charlotte—the poverty criterion would result in only a slightly larger number of eligible schools. In all districts the achievement-based method would lead to larger proportions of low-achieving students attending Title I schools.

Why are more schools (and therefore more students) eligible under the achievement than under the poverty criterion? Common sense suggests that low-achieving students are more evenly distributed across schools than are poor students. For example, fifteen of the twenty-eight schools in Racine have larger proportions of educationally disadvantaged students than the district average, while only ten of the schools have larger proportions of poor students than the district average (see Figure 7-1). Hence, the achievement criterion would qualify fifteen schools for Title I services in Racine, while the poverty criterion would qualify only ten.

We can measure the extent to which low achievers or poor students are concentrated in a relatively few schools by referring to skewness coefficients, which describe the shape of distributions. The coefficients indicate how low-achieving and poor students are distributed across schools in a district. A large positive coefficient means that most schools have relatively low proportions of students with a given characteristic, while a few schools have high proportions (as, for example, in the case of poverty in Racine). A zero coefficient describes a normal distribution, in which most schools fall in the

TABLE 7-6. SIMULATED EFFECTS OF SELECTING ALL ELEMENTARY SCHOOLS AT OR ABOVE DISTRICT AVERAGE PERCENT LOW-ACHIEVERS OR DISTRICT AVERAGE PERCENT POOR*

	PERCENTAGE ELEMENTARY SCHOOLS SELECTED BY:		PERCENTAGE OF DISTRICT LOW-ACHIEVERS ATTENDING SCHOOLS SELECTED BY:	
	Achievement	Poverty	Achievement	Poverty
DIRECT ALLOCATION DISTRICTS				
Adams County #12	63%	50%	77%	55%
Harrison County	48	48	48	46
Mesa	40	36	50	45
Newport	NA	NA	NA	NA
Racine	54	36	55	41
Santa Fe	50	44	57	55
ACHIEVEMENT ALLOCATION DISTRICTS				
Charlotte	50	52	61	49
Winston-Salem	54	46	72	57
OTHER DISTRICTS				
Alum Rock	56	44	56	43
Berkeley County	54	38	50	30
Boston	NA	NA	NA	NA
Houston	52	45	78	70
Yonkers	40	36	77	69
Mean	51	43	62	51

*Low-achieving students are defined as those reading one year or more below grade level.

Note: The measures of poverty and low achievement used to select schools vary from district to district. Data were not available for Newport and Boston.

middle range, having neither very high nor very low proportions of students with the characteristic in question. A large negative coefficient means that most schools have relatively high proportions of educationally disadvantaged or poor students, as the case may be.

FIGURE 7-1. DISTRIBUTIONS OF PERCENT OF LOW ACHIEVERS AND
PERCENT OF POOR ACHIEVERS IN RACINE

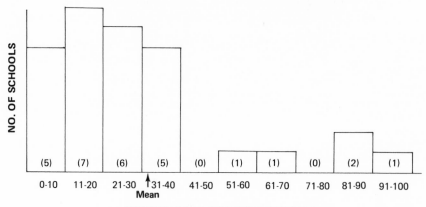

PERCENT POOR STUDENTS IN A SCHOOL

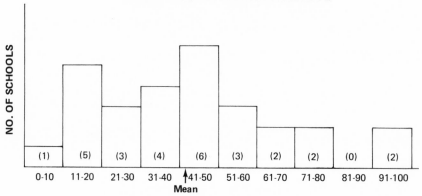

PERCENT LOW ACHIEVERS IN A SCHOOL

Skewness coefficients for the eleven districts in the simulation
clearly reveal that low-income students are more likely to be concentrated in a few schools than are low achievers. The mean coefficient
for the poverty distribution is .89, that for the low-achievement distribution is only.27; in ten of the eleven districts the poverty distribution showed greater skewness than did its counterpart. Thus, use
of the achievement criterion makes more schools eligible for Title I
services, because low achievers are more normally distributed throughout schools in the demonstration districts than are low-income
students.

Achievement- or Poverty-Based Allocation Among a Fixed Number of Students

In the above simulation it was assumed that the numbers of Title I schools in a district could vary according to the selection method used. But funding might be such that districts would prefer to hold the number of Title I schools constant, while allowing somewhat different schools to be selected depending upon the criterion.[4] An achievement or poverty criterion could be used to rank schools; the fixed number of schools having the highest rankings could then be selected. Table 7-7 shows the effects of achievement and poverty ranking on the numbers of educationally disadvantaged students in Title I schools.

The use of an achievement criterion with a fixed number of schools would result in slightly more educationally disadvantaged students having access to Title I services than would the use of poverty criteria. An average 65 percent of the districts' low achievers would have access using achievement ranking, 62 percent using poverty ranking. Seven of the eleven districts would have larger pools of disadvantaged students in schools selected on the basis of an achievement criterion, while two districts would have equal pools using the two criteria. However, in most of the seven districts the differences would be slight; in only two cases would they amount to more than 10 percent.[5]

CONCLUSION

Initially set up to help assess the effects of different allocation procedures, the Title I demonstration had a variety of consequences, some anticipated, some not. As expected, the districts expanded their programs, bringing Title I services to more schools and students than before. Contrary to expectation, however, they drew upon new resources to expand; they did not use the occasion of the demonstration to sharpen the focus of resources on the most disadvantaged. While more low-achieving students were served, the relative proportions of low achievers and other students receiving Title I services were largely unaltered.

Since the demonstration could not answer several important questions about the effects of specific allocation procedures, a number of simulations were conducted to explore the consequences of different strategies while holding other things constant. The simulations showed that (1) a perfectly efficient direct allocation system could

TABLE 7-7. SIMULATED EFFECTS OF SELECTING A CONSTANT
NUMBER OF ELEMENTARY SCHOOLS BY ACHIEVEMENT OR POVERTY
(NUMBER OF SCHOOLS EQUAL TO NUMBER SERVED
IN BASELINE YEAR)

	PERCENTAGE OF DISTRICT LOW-ACHIEVERS ATTENDING SCHOOLS SELECTED BY:	
	Achievement	Poverty
DIRECT ALLOCATION DISTRICTS		
Adams County #12	23%	26%
Harrison County	90	88
Mesa	62	62
Newport	NA	NA
Racine	50	50
Santa Fe	78	81
ACHIEVEMENT ALLOCATION DISTRICTS		
Charlotte	77	64
Winston-Salem	61	57
OTHER DISTRICTS		
Alum Rock	51	48
Berkeley County	92	80
Boston	NA	NA
Houston	56	51
Yonkers	70	69
Mean	65	62

Note: The measures of poverty and low achievement used to select schools vary from district to district. Data were not available for Newport and Boston.

provide coverage of the disadvantaged at least as good as that provided by the demonstration districts, which used additional resources to serve more students; (2) efficient and equitable targeting of funds within existing Title I schools could dramatically increase the number and proportion of educationally disadvantaged students served; (3) replacing poverty with low achievement as a school selection criterion could increase the percentage of low achievers with access to Title I services, if the number of schools was free to vary; but (4) if the number of schools was held constant, this increase would be minimal.

Notes

1. Conversely, perfect vertical equity could exist if *all* low achievers were served by Title I, as well as a number of less severely disadvantaged pupils (making the percentage of Title I students who were low achieving less than 100 percent). As we shall see in the remainder of this chapter, however, this situation is rare.

2. In contrast, there was a relatively consistent decline in the proportion of Title I students from low-income families. The mean decrease was 7 percent, with six districts showing significant losses.

3. A parallel analysis using low-income students as an outcome measure suggests that the average proportion of such students having access to Title I services would remain about the same under this achievement allocation method. In fact, in seven of the eleven districts it would result in larger percentages of low-income students having access.

4. Or, as in the rules pertaining to school targeting, Congress might set a ceiling on the number of schools which may qualify on the basis of achievement.

5. With respect to the proportion of low-income students in Title I schools according to the two criteria, the advantage would still lie with the poverty ranking. The pattern is one of moderate but consistent differences favoring the poverty criterion.

8

Effects of Alternative Allocation on the Services Students Receive

By revising their methods of allocation, the demonstration school districts were able to provide Title I services to an average of 74 percent more elementary school students than they had using the standard methods outlined in the regulations. The present chapter tells how this was achieved without any substantial loss of services to students. It is a story of creativity and flexibility in service delivery. That resources used to provide Title I services can be manipulated and organized in so many ways should be of particular interest to two groups: policymakers who fear the results of program deconcentration and practitioners who wish to serve more schools or students under current Title I regulations.

The thirteen demonstration districts received no additional Title I funds simply for participating in the study. How, then, did they manage to serve so many more students than they had before the demonstration? To answer this question, we investigated the methods which the districts used to select more students and the effects of increased selection on the compensatory services received by these students. We expected that the districts would cut back on the services offered each

147

student by substantially reducing either the quantity (that is, the amount of time) of compensatory instruction or its quality (for example, increasing class size or replacing reading specialists with teacher aides or classroom teachers), or both. However, we were wrong, our investigation showed that, on the contrary, services to students did not appreciably suffer.

Before presenting our findings, it should first be recognized that the provision of services to more students runs counter to the traditional notion that Title I services should be concentrated. According to the Title I regulations,

> Applications for grants ... or ... payments are to be concentrated on a limited number of projects and applied to a limited number of educationally deprived children so as to give reasonable promise of promoting to a marked degree improvement in the educational attainment, motivation, behavior, or attitudes of children.[1]

Thus, the regulations call for providing adequate services to a limited number of children rather than offering inadequate services to a larger number. An old OE program guideline (no longer in effect) further defined what was meant by concentration, stating that the per-student expenditure in Title I programs should be "about one-half the expenditure per child from State and local funds for the applicants' regular program."[2]

One might ask, Why have the concentration provision? What good does it do? First, Title I is intended to reach educationally deprived children, so it makes sense to concentrate resources on that group. Second, if resources are scarce, concentration of those resources seems reasonable. Rather than spreading limited funds across all eligible children or across a wide range of activities, it is logical to concentrate funds on those children who are most in need and on specific aspects of that need. Third, according to proponents of the "critical mass" concept in compensatory education, there is a monetary threshold which must be reached before a compensatory program can be effective.[3]

On the other hand, arguments can be made against the concentration provision. In a detailed analysis of the Title I program requirements, Silverstein points out several areas of ambiguity with respect to the concentration requirement.[4] For example, some of the language contained in the regulations is ambiguous, such as "sufficient concentration" and "a marked degree" of "improvement." Furthermore, the suggestion that concentration is achieved when Title I funds spent on each student are one-half the amount of state and local per-pupil funds appears to have no empirical basis. Certainly, it is not based on any research which relates dollars to educational performance.

The critical mass theory, although popular in the early days of Title I, is no longer widely believed. Research conducted over the past few years shows that while a base level of funding may be a necessary precondition for a compensatory program to have an effect on educational performance, it is by no means sufficient.[5] Averch et al. go so far as to speculate that in many cases educational expenditures may be reduced significantly without deterioration in educational outcomes.[6]

The notion of concentration also tends to be opposed by program administrators who, in Title I as in other service programs, are providing a service and would like that service to be available to as many needy children as possible. We have seen the way in which this conflict is resolved when the concentration provision is removed so that more or perhaps fewer children can be served (see chapter six). All the demonstration districts elected to increase the number of elementary school children served. The question remains, Did per-student compensatory services suffer because more students were served?

Before answering this question, consider again the amount and nature of compensatory instruction received by Title I elementary school students in the districts prior to the change in allocation policy (see chapter five for details). First, as would be expected, Title I students received more compensatory instruction than other students, about one-half hour more per day. Second, most compensatory instruction was in language arts and tended to be delivered in place of, rather than in addition to, regular classroom language arts instruction. As a result, the total amount of language arts instruction only slightly favored Title I over other students. Third, compensatory language arts was typically taught by reading specialists in small groups of students, while regular language arts was taught by classroom teachers in larger groups. It is against these baseline findings that changes in compensatory instruction are dicussed.

CHANGE IN AMOUNT OF INSTRUCTION

In most of the demonstration school districts students received slightly less compensatory language arts instruction after allocation policies were changed than they had previously. In most cases, these losses were accompanied by comparable or larger gains in regular language arts instruction (see Table 8-1).

TABLE 8-1. TIME SPENT IN COMPENSATORY LANGUAGE ARTS INSTRUCTION BY TITLE I STUDENTS

	TIME IN MINUTES PER DAY		CHANGE IN MINUTES	CHANGE AS PERCENTAGE OF BASELINE YEAR
	Baseline Year	Year One	Year One-Baseline Year	Year One-Baseline Year / Baseline Year
DIRECT ALLOCATION DISTRICTS				
Adams County #12	28	27	-1	-4%
Harrison County	28	30	2	7
Mesa	37	22	-15	-41
Newport	NA	NA	NA	NA
Racine	34	25	-9*	-26
Santa Fe	27	24	-3	-11
ACHIEVEMENT ALLOCATION DISTRICTS				
Charlotte	35	27	-8*	-23
Winston-Salem	41	41	0	0
OTHER DISTRICTS				
Alum Rock	41	31	-10	-24
Berkeley County	35	26	-9*	-26
Boston	41	34	-7	-17
Houston	38	34	-4	-11
Yonkers	30	33	3	10
Mean	35	30	-5	-14

*$p < .05$

Note: Because of small sample sizes, data for Newport were not included in this analysis.

Looking only at the direction of change in compensatory language arts, we find that in nine of the twelve districts for which data are available, Title I elementary school students spent less time in compensatory classes in the first year of the demonstration than they had in the baseline year. The average district loss is 5 minutes, or 14 percent of the instruction time prior to the demonstration. Data from reading specialists reveal that these losses were in part intentional. In eight of the eleven districts for which data are available, reading specialists planned a shorter instructional period. However, planned losses were generally smaller than actual losses (averaging only two minutes, or 7 percent of the baseline year amount). Therefore, it appears that Title I elementary school students lost some portion of their instructional time both at the planning and at the implementation stages of program delivery.

Although small losses in compensatory language arts were still evident in the second year of the demonstration, the average loss in service dropped from 14 percent to 7 percent. Thus, it appears that across time districts were able to restore some of the lost compensatory services.

Once again recalling findings from chapter five, note that compensatory language arts tends to replace rather than supplement regular language arts instruction. Thus, one would expect to find a reciprocal relationship between the two—if one goes down the other should go up. Since a fairly consistent loss was observed across districts in amount of compensatory language arts instruction delivered to Title I students, one would expect to see a corresponding increase in regular language arts. In nine of the school districts Title I elementary school children did receive more regular language arts instruction during the first year of the demonstration than they had previously (see Table 8-2). The increase averaged 15 minutes, or 16.8 percent of the amount in the baseline year. Only two districts went against the expected pattern, with Title I students spending less time in both compensatory and regular classroom language arts.

Thus, losses in amount of compensatory instruction were in most cases more than balanced by gains in amount of regular instruction. This supports the hypothesis of a reciprocal relationship between the two, although the relationship is not perfect. Actually, there is little reason to expect a perfect relationship between the two, considering the great differences in the nature of compensatory and regular instruction.

TABLE 8-2. TIME SPENT IN REGULAR LANGUAGE ARTS INSTRUCTION BY TITLE I STUDENTS

	TIME IN MINUTES PER DAY		CHANGE IN MINUTES	CHANGE AS PERCENTAGE OF YEAR ONE
	Baseline Year	Year One	Year One-Baseline Year	Year One-Baseline Year / Baseline Year
DIRECT ALLOCATION DISTRICTS				
Adams County #12	109	117	8	6%
Harrison County	120	117	-3	-3
Mesa	96	116	20*	17
Newport	NA	NA	NA	NA
Racine	112	124	12	11
Santa Fe	111	107	-4	-4
ACHIEVEMENT ALLOCATION DISTRICTS				
Charlotte	97	94	-3	-3
Winston-Salem	112	124	12*	10
OTHER DISTRICTS				
Alum Rock	68	95	27*	40
Berkeley	111	141	30*	27
Boston	90	106	16	18
Houston	122	145	23*	16
Yonkers	67	103	36*	54
Mean	101	116	15	16

*$p < .05$

Note: Because of small sample sizes, data for Newport were not included in this analysis.

CHANGE IN NATURE OF INSTRUCTION

The second measure of change in services specifies the nature of compensatory language arts instruction received by Title I elementary school students. Two aspects of instruction were defined in chapter five: the proportion of time spent by students in four different group sizes, and the proportion spent with four different types of instructors. (It should be noted that group size is always less than or equal to class size. If a compensatory class of twenty is divided into four working groups of equal size, the group size is five, not twenty.) Knowing that Title I elementary school students lost compensatory time when allocation policy was changed, one can ask whether the losses are spread equally over all group sizes and types of instructors. If proportionately less time is spent in small groups or with reading specialists, the special nature of the compensatory program will have been affected over and above the loss of time.[7]

Change in Group Size

Since the decrease in amount of compensatory language arts instruction received by each elementary school student in no way accounts for the increase in numbers of students served, we anticipated an increase in group size to offset program expansion. The data support this expectation: there was a slight shift toward the use of larger groups for the delivery of compensatory language arts instruction to Title I elementary school students. Prior to the demonstration students received compensatory instruction individually or in small groups 65 percent of the time. In the first year of the demonstration that figure was reduced to 60 percent, indicating an increase in the use of larger groups. At the district level, shifts of 20 percent or more are found only in three districts—toward smaller groups in one and toward larger groups in the other two (see Table 8-3). The size of compensatory language arts classes also increased during the first year of the demonstration by an average of 8 percent. Thus, both indicators—group size and class size—are consistent in direction and lead to the same conclusion—that one of the approaches used by the districts to offset the increase in number of elementary students served by Title I was to change the nature of the compensatory instruction received by those students.

TABLE 8-3. PERCENTAGE OF COMPENSATORY LANGUAGE ARTS DELIVERED IN INDIVIDUAL OR SMALL GROUPS

| | PERCENTAGE OF TIME SPENT IN INDIVIDUAL OR SMALL GROUPS | | CHANGE IN PERCENTAGE |
	Baseline Year	Year One	Year One- Baseline Year
DIRECT ALLOCATION DISTRICTS			
Adams County #12	37%	62%	25%
Harrison County	41	35	–6
Mesa	97	97	0
Newport	NA	NA	NA
Racine	100	99	–1
Santa Fe	83	81	–2
ACHIEVEMENT ALLOCATION DISTRICTS			
Charlotte	67	57	–10
Winston-Salem	55	64	9
OTHER DISTRICTS			
Alum Rock	72	61	–11
Berkeley County	71	44	–27
Boston	54	46	–8
Houston	32	34	2
Yonkers	68	38	–30
Mean	65	60	–5

Note: Because of small sample sizes, data for Newport were not included in this analysis.

While Title I elementary school students lost time in compensatory language arts, they gained it in regular language arts. Along with this increase in per-student time, there were changes in the size of the instructional group in which Title I students received regular language arts. Prior to the demonstration they received regular language arts instruction individually or in small groups only 29 percent of the time. During the demonstration this figure was reduced to 23 percent, indicating a small incease in the use of larger groups. Only two districts show sizable shifts, both of which indicate an increase in the proportion of time Title I elementary school students spent in larger groups.

Change in Type of Instructor

Considering the increase in numbers of students served by Title I elementary school programs, we expected either no change in type of instructor for compensatory language arts or less use of reading specialists. In general, however, there were only small changes in the type of compensatory language arts instructor. Table 8-4 shows that reading specialists delivered most of the compensatory instruction in both the baseline year and the first year of the demonstration. In the baseline year students in nine of twelve districts for which data were available received 60 percent or more of their compensatory language arts instruction from specialists; the first year of the demonstration showed an identical pattern. The two districts which had relied primarily on paraprofessionals before the demonstration continued to do so during it.

Few changes were expected or found in the type of regular language arts instructor. In the baseline year Title I elementary school students spent 73 percent of their time in regular language arts instruction with classroom teachers; during the demonstration the figure was 74 percent.

Since compensatory and regular language arts instruction differ considerably with respect to group size and type of instructor (see chapter five), we also searched for changes in these variables from the first year of the demonstration to the second. Overall there was no substantial dilution of compensatory services. There were only slight increases in group size and no changes in type of instructor.

With these results in mind we now return to the expectation set forth at the beginning of the chapter—that the loss in amount of compensatory language arts instruction received by each student would tend to balance the 74 percent increase in the number of elementary school students served. If so, it could be argued that the total amount of Title I compensatory instruction (the average amount of instruction per student multiplied by the number of participating elementary school students) remained stable over time. If so, the choice of alloca-

**TABLE 8-4. PERCENTAGE OF COMPENSATORY LANGUAGE ARTS
DELIVERED BY READING SPECIALISTS**

	PERCENTAGE OF TIME SPENT WITH READING SPECIALISTS		CHANGE IN PERCENTAGE
	Baseline Year	Year One	Year One- Baseline Year
DIRECT ALLOCATION DISTRICTS			
Adams County #12	83%	93%	10%
Harrison County	94	96	2
Mesa	22	17	-5
Newport	NA	NA	NA
Racine	11	10	-1
Santa Fe	82	79	-2
ACHIEVEMENT ALLOCATION DISTRICTS			
Charlotte	87	79	-8
Winston-Salem	81	68	-13
OTHER DISTRICTS			
Alum Rock	32	51	19
Berkeley County	62	76	14
Boston	88	74	-14
Houston	86	82	-4
Yonkers	67	88	21
Mean	66	68	2

Note: Because of small sample sizes, data for Newport were not included in this analysis.

tion strategy and the choice of whether or not to concentrate services—more students with less compensatory time per student, or fewer students with more time per student—might be considered purely a matter of district preference, with no net change in compensatory services across the population served. Of course, taken to the extreme, the quantity or quality of compensatory instruction delivered to each student could be so diminished as to be meaningless.

However, the average 14 percent loss in compensatory language arts time per student comes nowhere close to accounting for the 74 percent increase in number of students served. The small increase in group size and the negligible change in type of instructor offer little additional help in explaining the large increase in number of elementary school students participating in Title I. Perhaps changes in other factors could account for the ability of the districts to serve more elementary school students while keeping services per student at almost the same level.

CHANGE IN ELEMENTARY INSTRUCTIONAL EXPENDITURES

The large increase in total amount of compensatory instructional services observed at the elementary school level in the demonstration districts was supported in part by an increase in Title I expenditures for elementary school instruction. As shown in Table 8-5, districts increased expenditures for instruction 31 percent on average in the first year of the demonstration.[8] Since the districts were to receive no additional funds as remuneration for taking part in the demonstration, the large increase in elementary school expenditures shows how variable the normal flow of Title I funds is.[9] It also suggests the flexibility which districts have in using Title I funds for the provision of services.

Basically, the increase in Title I elementary school instructional expenditures came from three sources: (1) increases in the amount of funds allocated to the districts; (2) use of unspent funds carried over from the previous year; and (3) redistribution of district funds from other Title I programs to elementary school programs. The first two sources imply an overall increase in the amount of Title I funds expended during the demonstration. The latter implies no additional monies, but rather a shifting of priorities in the use of Title I dollars.

As noted earlier, Title I district allocations were not supposed to change simply as a result of participating in the demonstration. However, Title I allocations may change as a result of alterations in the poverty count within a district or across other districts in the same state, or as a result of redistribution within the state of unused monies. Also, if the total federal authorization is increased, the amount of funds received by a district will be increased, ceteris paribus. Title I

TABLE 8-5. TITLE I EXPENDITURES FOR ELEMENTARY SCHOOL INSTRUCTION

	EXPENDITURES IN DOLLARS		CHANGE AS PERCENTAGE OF BASELINE YEAR
	Baseline Year	Year One	Year One-Baseline Year / Baseline Year
DIRECT ALLOCATION DISTRICTS			
Adams County #12	$ 78,520	$ 151,312	93%
Harrison County	359,370	506,510	41
Mesa	180,431	177,455	-2
Newport	129,288	274,530	112
Racine	417,679	791,838	90
Santa Fe	395,437	433,082	10
ACHIEVEMENT ALLOCATION DISTRICTS			
Charlotte	2,279,136	2,304,284	1
Winston-Salem	766,711	1,187,617	55
OTHER DISTRICTS			
Alum Rock	912,187	898,054	-2
Berkeley County	249,760	254,704	2
Boston	6,199,829	6,854,229	11
Houston	4,611,342	5,442,133	18
Yonkers	1,606,615	1,175,645	-27
Mean			31

Note: These figures exclude costs for summer school.

allocations in the demonstration district increased 5 percent on average during the first year of the demonstration and another 13 percent during the second. Furthermore, although three districts experienced small reductions in year one, all districts had increments during year two. Thus, the increase in allocations was generally sizable and uniform.

While it is not possible to link increased Title I allocations to inflationary trends in unit costs, such trends would certainly lessen the impact of increased allocations on service expansion. In the demonstration districts, for example, the average increase in allocations from the baseline year to the second year of the demonstration (18 percent) was less than the average increase in unit costs for specialists' salaries (23 percent). In fact, district administrators report that they view increased allocations, at least in part, as a hedge against inflation.

A second potential source of increased elementary school expenditures is the existence of "carry-over funds." This term refers to any unspent portion of funds from the previous year's allocation. The origin of carry-over funds can be traced to the Nixon administration's decision to impound federal funds in the late 1960s and early 1970s. Districts responded by underspending their Title I allocations. The resulting backup fund could be used in part for expenditures made before Title I funds were received and in part as a hedge against the possibility of reduced funding. What was a short-term response to a problem has now become an established part of program operations, and carry-over funds can represent a fairly large supply of money for use in meeting immediate expenditures. In fact, funds carried over into the demonstration represented an average 35 percent of total Title I expenditures in the thirteen districts.

In the eleven districts where data were available, carry-over funds were depleted in both demonstration years (see Table 8-6). Carry-over depletion associated with year one (when the greatest increases in both services and instructional expenditures were made) was almost double that found in the baseline year. Finally, a comparison of carry-over out of the demonstration with carry-over into the demonstration indicates that, on the average, the eleven districts depleted 60 percent of their carry-over funds during the demonstration.

Effective use of carry-over funds would seem to require that their "one-shot" nature be matched by a one-shot resource purchase. Just as one of the basic tenets of financing in the business world is to match short-term debt with short-term expected returns (for example, inventories), so it would seem important to match the expenditure of carry-over funds to one-shot investments (for example, the expense of setting up reading labs in new Title I schools or the purchase of

TABLE 8-6. PERCENTAGE CHANGE IN TITLE I CARRY-OVER FUNDS*

	CHANGE IN BASELINE YEAR	CHANGE IN YEAR ONE**
DIRECT ALLOCATION DISTRICTS		
Adams County #12	40%	-42%
Harrison County	135	-53
Mesa	-61	93
Newport	32	-52
Racine	-36	-50
Santa Fe	-43	-8
ACHIEVEMENT ALLOCATION DISTRICTS		
Charlotte	-16.4	19.8
Winston-Salem	-12.8	-25.7
OTHER DISTRICTS		
Alum Rock	-53.7	-20.7
Berkeley County	NA	NA
Boston	-39.0	-97.2
Houston	NA	NA
Yonkers	-61.3	-27.4
Mean	-10.5	-20.7

*The change in carry-over funds for a given year represents the carry-over into the following year, minus the carry-over into the given year, divided by the carry-over into the given year.

**The average change in year two was -23.

Note: Data are not provided for Berkeley County since no carry-over funds were available, and data are not provided for Houston since carry-over funds were used almost exclusively for the summer school program.

audiovisual teaching machines, which might allow more students to receive Title I services). With the possible exception of Winston-Salem, which increased expenditures for audiovisual equipment, most districts spent the increased monies on recurring-cost resources (for example, reading specialists). Thus, the depletion of carry-over funds during the demonstration may have serious implications for maintaining increased service levels.

The third source of increased elementary school instructional expenditures, redistribution of resources, had no impact on total Title I expenditures—the size of the local pie remained unchanged. However, a larger slice of that pie went to elementary school instructional expenditures.

The proportion of total Title I expenditures allocated to elementary school instruction increased from 70 percent in the year preceding the demonstration to 80.2 percent in the first year of it (in the second year the increase was 82 percent). These large gains in the concentration of resources at the elementary school level were balanced by losses in other Title I components. Of the three districts which show the largest gains in elementary school resources, two eliminated Title I secondary school instruction and one of those two eliminated Title I kindergarten programs.

An important determinant in the districts' decisions to eliminate or reduce other Title I components was the existence of other compensatory programs in the district. Generally, programs which were eliminated from Title I funding the first year of the demonstration were subsequently funded by local, state, or other federal compensatory programs. Thus, Title I losses were seldom translated into real losses.

We can get an idea of how these fiscal strategies may have permitted service expansion by relating baseline characteristics to actual increases in students served. Districts differed, for example, in their treatment of carry-over funds (see Table 8-7). The three districts in Group I accumulated carry-over funds in the baseline year and then depleted them in year one. Put another way, the three districts underspent their allocations in the baseline year and overspent their allocations in year one. The opposite pattern—depletion in the baseline year and accumulation in year one—was exhibited by three other districts (Group II). Comparing changes in the number of students served, we see that Group I districts increased the number of students served in year one an average of 139 percent, almost seven times the average increase found in Group II districts. Thus, it appears that the accumulation-depletion pattern exhibited by the first group of districts may have helped them expand services.

Not all districts were able to use another strategy—redistribution of resources (see Table 8-8). For example, districts whose Title I

TABLE 8-7. TREATMENT OF CARRY-OVER FUNDS AND PERCENTAGE CHANGE IN ELEMENTARY SCHOOL STUDENTS SERVED

	PERCENTAGE CHANGE IN ELEMENTARY SCHOOL STUDENTS YEAR ONE
GROUP I DISTRICTS	
Adams County #12	263
Harrison County	32
Newport	121
Mean	139
GROUP II DISTRICTS	
Mesa	32
Charlotte	11
Yonkers	20
Mean	21

Note: Group I districts accumulated carry-over funds in the baseline year and depleted them in year one; Group II districts showed the opposite pattern.

funds were spent entirely on elementary school instruction would have no funds left to redistribute to this component of Title I. This was the situation faced by the five districts in Group A, which had the highest allocation of funds to elementary school instruction in the year preceding the demonstration. Group B includes the five districts with the lowest baseline year allocation of funds to elementary school instruction. Group A districts increased the number of elementary students served by an average of 49 percent; the equivalent figure for Group B is 122 percent. Thus, it would appear that the potential for redistribution of total Title I funds helped determine the magnitude of service expansion possible at the elementary level.

TABLE 8-8. ALLOCATION OF TITLE I FUNDS AND PERCENTAGE CHANGE IN ELEMENTARY SCHOOL STUDENTS SERVED

	PERCENTAGE OF FUNDS SPENT ON ELEMENTARY INSTRUCTION BASELINE YEAR	PERCENTAGE CHANGE IN ELEMENTARY STUDENTS SERVED YEAR ONE
GROUP A DISTRICTS		
Alum Rock	100%	134%
Berkeley County	95	50
Charlotte	94	10
Harrison County	94	32
Yonkers	92	20
Mean		49
GROUP B DISTRICTS		
Racine	40	111
Mesa	44	32
Newport	49	121
Winston-Salem	50	84
Adams County #12	52	263
Mean		122

DONATED RESOURCES

In addition to using Title I allocations and carry-over funds, many schools relied on resources donated either by the district or by other compensatory programs. Donated resources can take many forms; the most common is space provided by the district for Title I instruction. Principals' time spent coordinating Title I activities at the school level is another form of district-donated resource. In some districts instructional specialists and aides are also donated. For example, Mesa's Title I program funds aides, while the district donates specialists. Finally, instructional supplies and materials may be donated.

Donated resources are as important as Title I allocations in purchasing services, since in most cases the loss of these resources would require replacement with Title I funds. Given the 74 percent increase in number of elementary school students served during the demonstration, we would expect the amount of donated resources at least to remain constant. The figures displayed in Table 8-9 verify this expectation; the value of donated resources has generally kept pace with increases in the amount of elementary school instructional expenditures.

While eleven districts made some use of donated resources, only in two districts were such resources a substantial proportion of all costs in both the year preceding and the first year of the demonstration. In both years Mesa relied on donated resources from the local educational agency, while Berkeley County relied on such resources from the federal Emergency School Aid Assistance (ESAA) program. The remaining districts that used substantial amounts of donated resources (Adams County #12 in the baseline year and Newport in year one) provide an interesting contrast. Adams County #12 decided to formalize local compensatory efforts which had supplemented Title I during the baseline year. The new program served grades which were no longer served by Title I; the resources previously donated to the Title I program were allocated instead to this program. Newport, on the other hand, provided Title I, state, and local resources to students in elementary schools during the baseline year. With the pooling of resources and services for all elementary school grades in year one, the use of donated resources increased. In a sense, the real change in these two districts is not in their reliance on donated resources so much as in the coordination of Title I with other programs. (See chapter nine for a discussion of coordination among various compensatory education programs.)

OTHER EXPANSION STRATEGIES

An important question remains: Can a school district which does not receive an increased Title I allocation, which has no carry-over funds, which has no potential for redistribution of total Title I funds, and which receives no donated resources find ways to expand elementary school Title I services? The demonstration illustrates that districts can use nonfiscal strategies in order to support program expansion.

TABLE 8-9. DONATED RESOURCES AND TOTAL COSTS

| | RATIO OF ESTIMATED VALUE DONATED RESOURCES TO TOTAL COSTS | |
	Baseline Year	Year one
DIRECT ALLOCATION DISTRICTS		
Adams County #12	48	1
Harrison County	1	1
Mesa	55	56
Newport	8	23
Racine	1	1
Santa Fe	7	3
ACHIEVEMENT ALLOCATION DISTRICTS		
Charlotte	1	8
Winston-Salem	12	12
OTHER DISTRICTS		
Alum Rock	NA	NA
Berkeley County	27	31
Boston	5	6
Houston	3	6
Yonkers	NA	NA
Mean (11 sites)	15	13
(9 sites without Adams County and Newport)	12	14

Note: Total costs equal donated resources plus elementary school instructional expenditures. These data were not available for Alum Rock and Yonkers.

One such strategy has already been discussed: dilution of services through increased class size. For example, Harrison County increased class size in compensatory language arts instruction from eight to ten students, thereby enabling the program to serve 25 percent more students. The only additional expenditures required for this expansion were for instructional materials and supplies. It is conceivable that districts might have pursued this strategy further; however, as we noted in chapter five, it may impinge on the quality of instruction.

A second strategy involving dilution of services would change the mix of specialists and aides. Since at the time of the demonstration the average salary of a specialist was 2.86 times larger than the average salary of an aide, districts could have expanded services to an extent greater than expenditures would allow by concentrating resources on aides. But, as we have seen, although districts were willing to increase class size in order to expand services, they did not change the type of instructor. In fact, the average ratio of specialists to instructional personnel actually increased slightly in the first year of the demonstration. (Three districts decreased the specialist-instructional personnel ratio in year one.)

A third strategy used to expand services was to increase the number of hours that the specialist spent in direct instruction, as opposed to administrative, training, or other activities. Seven of the nine districts for which data were available increased the amount of direct instruction provided by language arts specialists in year one by an average of 10 percent (see Table 8-10). This increase in use of specialists at the elementary school level is all the more notable when we consider that the number of elementary school specialists (and therefore the number of specialists potentially new to the Title I program) increased an average of 34 percent in year one. If some of these new staff members were first-time specialists, they would have required more in-service training and more preparation time than experienced specialists. Furthermore, even experienced specialists new to the Title I program may have required familiarization with the instructional approaches and materials used in the program. Thus, the fact that specialists spent more time providing direct instruction in year one suggests that the districts deliberately increased staff utilization in order to expand services. In addition to the number of hours spent in direct instruction, there was a slight increase in the number of hours specialists spent diagnosing and prescribing instruction for students. In contrast to these increases, the percentage of specialists' time spent in preparation and record keeping generally declined.

SUMMARY AND CONCLUSION

In summary, we have seen that the demonstration school districts were able to serve many more elementary school students with only

TABLE 8-10. DIRECT INSTRUCTION PROVIDED BY SPECIALISTS

	TIME IN HOURS PER WEEK		CHANGE AS PERCENTAGE OF BASELINE YEAR
			Year One-Baseline Year
	Baseline Year	Year One	Baseline Year
DIRECT ALLOCATION DISTRICTS			
Adams County #12	22	26	18
Harrison County	22	23	5
Mesa	NA	NA	NA
Newport	18	18	0
Racine	12	14	17
Santa Fe	16	22	38
ACHIEVEMENT ALLOCATION DISTRICTS			
Charlotte	21	21	0
Winston-Salem	20	21	5
OTHER DISTRICTS			
Alum Rock	NA	NA	NA
Berkeley County	23	NA	NA
Boston	22	22	0
Houston	22	24	9
Yonkers	NA	NA	NA
Mean			10

Note: These data were not available for four districts.

a slight decrease in services per student. Although there was some loss in compensatory language arts instruction, there was a corresponding increase in regular language arts instruction. Instructional group (and class) size increased somewhat, but there was no change in type of instructor.

The districts were able to avoid cutting elementary school Title I services mainly because they devoted more resources to elementary school education. Increased allocations, depletion of carry-over funds, targeting of available Title I funds, and increased use of donated resources all help explain how this was accomplished.

Though other strategies can be employed which allow service expansion without a concomitant increase in expenditures, there are often trade-offs in terms of the quality of such services. In expanding class size there is a potential loss in terms of individualization of instruction. In changing the specialist-aide mix there is a potential loss in the quality of instruction provided to compensatory students. Finally, in increasing the amount of instruction provided by specialists there are losses in the time spent by specialists in other activities. However, students may well benefit from this particular trade-off.

Notes

1.   45 C.F.R. 116.18 (e) (1974).

2.   *Program Guide No. 44,* Section 4.7.

3.   W. Doherty, "Critical Mass in Compensatory Education," paper presented at the annual meeting of the American Educational Research Association, San Francisco, Calif., 1976.

4.   NIE, *Administration of Compensatory Education.*

5.   Doherty, "Critical Mass."

6.   Harvey A. Averch et al., *How Effective is Schooling? A Critical Review and Synthesis of Findings* (Santa Monica, Calif.: Rand Corporation, 1972).

7.   In this discussion we present findings in terms of proportion of time rather than in minutes. This allows an assessment of change in group size and type of instructor over and above the changes in amount of instruction already noted.

8.   Average elementary school expenditures increased an additional 11 percent from the first to the second year of the demonstration and were 43 percent higher in the second year than in the baseline year.

9.   Each district did receive a small grant to cover additional costs incurred because of administrative and data collection responsibilities, but these funds were not used to provide Title I services.

9

The Demonstration District Experience: Policy Questions and Practical Problems

The districts involved in the demonstration were expected to serve as working models of the specific changes in Title I allocation policy considered by Congress during the 1974 deliberations. We have already described the effects of those allocation changes on the characteristics of Title I services. In addition to these basic findings, the demonstration unexpectedly shed some light on three concerns of considerable importance to Title I. Emerging from the regulatory structure and administration of the program, as well as from congressional debates leading to the demonstration, these concerns are that (1) local autonomy may result in abuses of the program and thus must be curtailed, (2) the use of achievement criteria for allocating money to schools may give rise to disincentives, and (3) districts may not give parents a significant role in the governance of Title I.

In this chapter we discuss the insights provided by the demonstration into each of these concerns. We shall see that, far from abusing the local autonomy granted by the demonstration waivers, the districts succeeded in using the occasion of the demonstration to plan and implement sound, well-coordinated compensatory education programs serving larger numbers of children. We shall also see that there are counter pressures which serve to reduce the disincentives associated with achievement-based allocation of Title I dollars. Finally, we shall see that while some districts resist parent participation in Title I, others find effective vehicles for involving parents in program design and implementation.[1]

THE ISSUE OF LOCAL AUTONOMY

From the beginning, the Title I legal framework has set limits on the autonomy of local districts with regard to the use of Title I funds. The rules have been increasingly tightened over the life of the program to safeguard federal monies from local encroachment. They require not only that funds be targeted for educationally disadvantaged children in schools serving low-income areas, but also that the compensatory services provided be supplementary to those regularly provided by the district.

Implicit in this legal framework is a judgment on the part of the federal government that local districts, left to their own devices, would divert Title I funds to provide local tax relief or for general aid. Given the burgeoning taxpayers' revolt, this is not at all an unreasonable assumption. As noted in chapter three, districts are under strong pressure to use Title I funds for general or emergency needs.

Just how stringently does this legal framework actually restrict district autonomy? Within the basic constraints, it actually allows the districts considerable flexibility in planning and implementing their Title I programs. In addition, federal administration of Title I is not as intensive as a simple reading of the regulations might imply. There are those who argue that in practice local school districts have the final say in the spending of Title I funds.[2]

As discussed in chapter three, however, many districts are not aware of the extent of the flexibility and autonomy that Title I actually offers. Under the supervision of their state educational agencies, they often perceive the rules governing Title I as extremely strict and limiting. Thus, in an attempt to comply with excessively stringent interpretations of the requirements governing the distribution of Title I funds, districts often define their programs narrowly, choosing safety over innovation and creativity.

The demonstration offered participating districts increased autonomy in two respects. First, waivers of the eligibility and concentration requirements provided a *real* relaxation of external control.

Second, and perhaps even more important, the general atmosphere of the demonstration itself provided a *perception* of increased local autonomy on the part of the districts. Out of this situation came changes in the use of resources that were quite dramatic.

Before we proceed to our discussion of these changes, one caveat is in order. It might be argued that the demonstration districts were in reality subjected to far greater federal management than usual. While the formal regulations regarding concentration and school selection were indeed relaxed, participating districts were highly visible to federal administrators at NIE, who were very aware of general Title I program requirements. District plans for the demonstration were carefully scrutinized and reviewed prior to approval. Furthermore, throughout the demonstration the participating districts were closely monitored by both state and NIE personnel and were subject to intensive research. All this attention probably made the districts unusually conscious of and careful about complying with Title I program regulations.

Thus, we are not suggesting that federal management was abdicated or even loosened under the demonstration; in fact, if anything, the federal presence was intensified. What is different and significant, however, is that service distribution decisions were allowed to proceed more from the bottom up (from the perspective of local needs and desires) than from the top down (from the perspective of legal program requirements or restrictive interpretations of those requirements).

The changes in the use of resources that came out of this context were of two types, those involving largely internal changes in Title I programs and those involving coordination between Title I and other compensatory programs. Internal changes in resource distribution were discussed at length in chapter eight and are of interest to us at this point chiefly to illustrate how the districts reacted to their perceptions of increased local autonomy.

Few of the changes described in chapter eight were dependent upon the waiver of any particular regulation. The districts could have reallocated internal program resources in several ways. For example, under the normal Title I regulations they could have eliminated educational services in the secondary schools in order to expand services in the elementary schools. However, it was only during the demonstration that they chose to do so.

Two factors appear to have prompted the districts to respond to the demonstration in this fashion. Certainly the opportunity offered by the demonstration waivers to serve more students in more schools (but with the same amount of money) prompted the search for better ways of using existing program funds. But more important than this stimulus was the fact that, for the first time since the beginning of Title I the districts felt free—and indeed were directed—to conduct an intensive reassessment of Title I and compensatory education goals and resource allocation.

Over the years Title I has grown substantially and somewhat haphazardly. From the district perspective funding has often been unpredictable. Furthermore, regulations and program requirements have been refined and extended in a piecemeal fashion with excessively strict interpretations often resulting. In response to this pattern, districts have usually added program components and services as funds permitted and the most apparent needs dictated, without conducting a comprehensive assessment of compensatory education goals and resource allocation. An analogy might be that of a homeowner who over the years has remodeled or tacked on a room here and there as funds and zoning regulations permitted, ending up with a house that, while livable, does not fully or most efficiently meet the owner's needs. For the participating districts, the demonstration provided an opportunity to stand back and look at their compensatory education house for the first time.

Two excellent illustrations of this reassessment are Harrison County, West Virginia, and Houston, Texas. Both of these districts found the demonstration an occasion to make some dramatic internal changes in procedures that had emerged from their particular experiences with Title I and become solidified as "the way Title I is."

Harrison County had gradually developed a popular and costly Title I summer school program. The program had grown to its predemonstration size because of the planning difficulties associated with unpredictable variations in Title I allocations and because of federal controversy in the early 1970s concerning the legitimacy of carrying over funds. Essentially, funding the summer school program allowed the district to spend, rather than return unspent, unanticipated increases in Title I allocations without endangering the stability of the core Title I program. In other words, once the basic elementary school reading program was securely established, any unexpected increases in allocation could be used for an expanded summer school program. Since Title I summer programs tend to be regarded as luxuries rather than necessities, changes in the scope or size of the program from year to year were acceptable to both administrators and parents.

The summer program in Harrison County was so well received that it grew from a money-spending mechanism to a highly successful and prominent part of the Title I program. In fact, it was the subject of considerable pride and satisfaction among both administrators and parents.

Regardless of its success, however, the summer program had not been designed as an integral part of an educational package, but more or less "grew like Topsy." Under the stimulus of the demonstration, the district took a hard look at this program and eliminated it in favor of expanding Title I services during the regular year. It should be noted that Title I parents participated fully in this decision and voted positively on the direct question.

In Houston the demonstration presented a unique opportunity to challenge the state's overly strict interpretations of regulations. Prior to (and during) the demonstration, Houston operated a large and complex Title I program. In 1975-76, for example, the program funded thirteen separate components (some of which were further subdivided into discrete activities) in sixty schools. Under the state department's particularly strict interpretation of the Title I concentration regulation, the district was required to concentrate these components in targeted schools according to each school's poverty ranking. In essence, the highest-ranked schools had to be saturated with Title I program components before the lower-ranked schools could be served.

According to district administrators, this system presented serious space and scheduling problems for school personnel. Furthermore, school staff protested that often a particular student did not need one component but could use more units of another component. Given the state educational agency's particular interpretation of the concentration regulation, however, district administrators could not be responsive to these complaints.

During the demonstration Houston received a waiver of the state concentration regulations. Under this waiver the district adopted a "market basket" approach to distribution of funds for its Title I program. Distribution was calculated by multiplying the number of students served in a school by the district expenditure per student. For example, 100 students at $300 per student entitled a school to $30,000. Using these funds, the principal, teachers, and Title I parents together could select and purchase the particular Title I program components they felt were most appropriate for their particular school. For example, one school might choose to concentrate on reading and hence purchase several units of the Title I reading component. Another might decide that reading is largely under control and choose to concentrate its Title I dollars on early childhood and math units. The menu of components, along with their associated costs per unit, was provided by Title I district administrators. The components per se were virtually the same as in previous years. The district also provided assistance in selecting components and planning school programs as desired.

This approach was so well received that Houston, with the full support of the state educational agency, continued it after the demonstration ended. In essence, the demonstration experience led the state department to refine its interpretation of the concentration regulation (at least in the case of Houston).

Certainly one could argue that both Harrison County and Houston could have made these internal changes at any time; they did not have to wait for the demonstration for permission. Nevertheless, whether accurately or not, the districts perceived themselves as having substantially greater local autonomy, freedom, and flexibility than usual under the demonstration. They took advantage of this opportunity to initiate comprehensive and bold changes in response to local conditions. These changes did not result in an abuse of federal objectives, but rather in the more efficient use of resources. Thus, the demonstration raises serious questions about the effects of both perceived and actual restrictiveness in the Title I legal framework on district program design.

When we look at the changes made by some districts in external resource allocation, that is, changes in the way Title I was coordinated with other compensatory programs, we see a similar pattern. In contrast to the internal changes, however, these external changes were dependent upon the *real* increases in local autonomy provided by the demonstration—the eligibility and concentration waivers. In effect the demonstration districts used the waivers for the purpose of developing comprehensive compensatory education programs. Needless to say, the districts achieved results that they believed were highly beneficial to their overall compensatory effort.

Before discussing these external changes, it is necessary to describe current rules governing the coordination of Title I and state and local compensatory funds. As noted in chapter two, districts are permitted to coordinate the distribution of Title I and other compensatory education funds. However, the educationally deprived children in areas eligible for Title I assistance must, as a group, receive their "fair share" (as determined by state or local law) of other compensatory education funds. Districts can design and implement coordinated programs in a number of ways. They may use Title I funds to pay for different services to the same children. For example, Title I may be used to pay for a reading program while other compensatory funds support a math program. Alternatively, Title I and other compensatory monies may be used to pay for the same services to different children; for example, to children in different grade spans or to different sets of children within the same grade span. Under still another scenario, a Title I-eligible school may be skipped and other compensatory funds provided to that school, if the latter provide educationally deprived children in those schools with services of the same nature and scope as would have been provided under Title I.

On the surface, these rules appear to give the districts a great deal of flexibility in program design. In reality, however, the fair share requirement places a serious restriction on the use of state and local compensatory funds and overall program coordination. A hypothetical example will make this clear. In a certain school district, with ten schools, five are eligible for Title I assistance. Using the 50th percentile as a criterion for student eligibility, the district identifies 450 students in the ten schools as educationally disadvantaged; 300 of them attend Title I schools. If a more stringent criterion—one year or more below grade level—is used, 300 children qualify for compensatory services, and of these, 200 are in Title I schools (see Figure 9-1).

Title I funds for the district total $100,000. Given a per-pupil expenditure of $500, the district is able to serve 200 students with these monies. State and local compensatory funds total $75,000; an additional 150 children can be served using this funding source. Since 300 (two-thirds) of the 450 educationally deprived children in the district attend Title I schools, to comply with fair share requirements, two-thirds of the state and local funds must be spent in these schools.

This district has a number of alternatives in distributing its Title I and other compensatory education funds. Assuming it wishes to use the less severe definition of low achievement, it may consider any child who scores below the 50th percentile on a standardized test as eligible for compensatory services. The district can serve 200 of the 300 children eligible under this criterion with its Title I funds. By using other state and local funds, it can serve an additional 100 eligible students in Title I schools, plus 50 extra students in non-Title I schools. Thus, in this instance, Title I and other funds combine to serve all those eligible in Title I schools and more.

However, assume that the district wants to focus Title I monies on the severely disadvantaged and use other compensatory funds to distribute services to all schools in the district. If the district uses the

**FIGURE 9-1. DISTRIBUTION OF LOW ACHIEVERS AMONG
TEN SCHOOLS IN A HYPOTHETICAL DISTRICT**

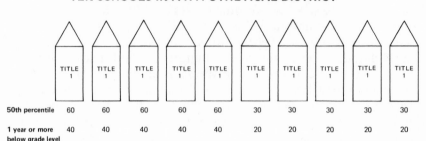

50th percentile	60	60	60	60	60	30	30	30	30	30
1 year or more below grade level	40	40	40	40	40	20	20	20	20	20

more stringent criterion described above, all of the 200 students eligible for Title I services in Title I schools can be served with Title I monies.

While no additional funds are needed, the district must spend two-thirds of its other compensatory funds in these schools, either by adding to existing services or by lowering the cutoff level (in direct contrast to the district's goal). Under any scenario, only 50 of the 100 severely disadvantaged students in non-Title I schools can be served given a fixed expenditure of $500 per child.

Thus, the requirements governing distribution of Title I funds not only prevent use of those funds to serve educationally deprived children in non-Title I schools, they also limit the use of state and local funds for this purpose. As a result, districts may simply be unable to serve the neediest students in all their schools.

During the demonstration most districts continued their previous approaches to interprogram coordination and simply tightened things up a bit. However, two districts—Adams County #12 and Newport—used their new funds allocation autonomy in conjunction with interprogram coordination to make sweeping and dramatic changes. Both districts were able to use the waivers and innovative coordination mechanisms to provide, for the first time, a comprehensive, district-wide compensatory education package.

In the year preceding the demonstration, Adams County #12 was providing reading, mathematics instruction, and special education to 174 elementary school students in three public schools, as well as offering reading (and some math) instruction to a number of secondary school students. Under direct allocation the number of elementary schools served in 1976-77 increased to 16 (the total number in the district at that time), and the number of elementary students served increased to 591. Total elementary school expenditures were $151,312 in 1976-77, compared to the previous year's $78,520.

How did Adams County #12 accomplish this? First, the decision was made to focus Title I services on the improvement of reading skills; the math component was dropped. Then the district adopted an early intervention strategy and installed Title I services only in grades one, two, and three. In order to ensure that children would not lose the reading gains they had made, the district hired eight elementary and nine secondary school compensatory specialists to serve children in grades four through twelve. Prior to the demonstration the district had hired a few such specialists in an effort to supplement Title I. During the demonstration this local effort was formalized and considerably extended.

The net result of this reorganization and coordination of services was a comprehensive, districtwide compensatory education program. The use of Title I funds in grades one through three allowed the district to provide intensive services to the most educationally disadvantaged children everywhere in the district during their first years of schooling. By using local compensatory services in grades four through twelve, the district could follow these children throughout their entire school experience and provide additional intervention as needed.

It is safe to say that the increase in funds allocation autonomy provided by the demonstration was the major impetus for development of this program. The waivers gave the district the opportunity to provide intensive instruction for all of the most educationally disadvantaged children in the elementary schools. This in turn stimulated the district to find funds from several different sources to extend and formalize the local compensatory effort. In short, during the demonstration Adams County #12 saw for the first time an opportunity to provide a comprehensive program. In the words of district administrators, "far from supplanting the district effort, the allowance to combine both the Title I and district effort has provided for the most complete compensatory program Adams County School District #12 has ever had."

For Adams County #12, the end of the demonstration spelled an end to its comprehensive program and a consequent reduction in services. A return to the previous school eligibility criterion (poverty) has meant that only seven elementary schools are eligible for Title I services. As a result, ten schools (one new school was opened during the demonstration) have lost Title I funds. Furthermore, under the fair share requirement, the local compensatory effort cannot fully replace Title I in these schools. As the district administrators observed, "Instead of serving 55 percent of the bottom [25th] quartile for all district students in grades one, two, and three, services will undoubtedly be extended to all students in the bottom [25th] quartile for only seven schools plus a certain percentage below the 50th percentile in these same schools in a different program area, i.e., language arts instead of reading."

Of course, both parents and teachers at the ten ineligible schools, as well as the district administrators, are extremely unhappy about the situation. When asked to list the benefits of the demonstration, Adams County #12 personnel listed first "the coordination of district financial support with Title I"; the second benefit was that "Title I children moving within the district could be serviced by any school." Due to the rapid growth of the area, children are extremely mobile within this district. The possibility of addressing this problem of mobility was one of the district's stated reasons for participating in the demonstration.

Newport illustrates a somewhat different approach to the coordination of a comprehensive, districtwide effort. In this case the coordination was between Title I and a state (and local) compensatory program. Once again, however, this coordination grew out of the district's desire to serve low-achieving students in all elementary schools, which, given the fair share requirement, was not possible outside the demonstration.

Like Adams County #12, Newport used direct allocation, and in the first year of the demonstration it served almost twice as many elementary school students as it had in the preceding year. Prior to the demonstration, Newport's state compensatory program, "Section 4" (which also received local funds) focused exclusively on reading, as did Title I. Section 4 served grades one through three in all elementary schools, while Title I served grades four through six only in Title I-eligible schools. The two programs overlapped administratively and were designed to provide a complementary spectrum of services.

Until Newport's voluntary desegregation in 1974, these coordinated programs had reached almost all of the most severely disadvantaged students in grades four through six, who were clustered in the Title I schools. With desegregation, however, these children were scattered throughout the district. As a consequence of Title I eligibility requirements, only three elementary schools qualified for services.

Thus, many of the children who had received services in grades one through three under Section 4 were deprived of them in grades four through six.

Newport saw the demonstration as an opportunity to design a continuous program. The district perceived that the demonstration waivers made it possible to integrate both the Section 4 and Title I programs at all elementary school grade levels. By so doing, the district could operate a single compensatory reading program serving students in grades one through six.

Newport considered this single program so successful that it encouraged other demonstration districts to join Newport in a united effort to extend the waivers beyond the two-year demonstration period. Newport applied for the extension in the belief that, were waivers refused and the district forced to go back to the old mode of operation, the compensatory effort would be seriously weakened.

What was it about the demonstration that made these changes in Newport and Adams County #12 possible? For both districts, the funds allocation waivers allowed expansion of Title I services to all elementary schools. Without the waivers both districts would have been required to concentrate funds on students within Title I schools, including some students with only moderate needs. The waivers allowed the districts to serve greater numbers of extremely disadvantaged students throughout the district.

The results of the demonstration lead to the following conclusions about local autonomy. First, within the context of providing services to disadvantaged children, greater district autonomy in funds allocation does not necessarily lead to program abuse. In fact, as Adams County #12 and Newport illustrate, it may well lead to improved services for more educationally disadvantaged students. Second, as Harrison County and Houston illustrate, districts are not making full use of the considerable autonomy and flexibility that the regulations actually allow. Whatever the reasons, the demonstration results support the perception that state and local jurisdictions often adopt a better-safe-than-sorry philosophy which may discourage innovation and hinder efficient use of resources.

THE ISSUE OF DISINCENTIVES

A second concern with Title I is the possibility that it creates disincentives. This issue, which is more philosophical than legal, was frequently raised in the political debate surrounding the 1974 Amendments. Those who opposed providing funds to schools on the basis of achievement argued that achievement-based allocation rewards low achievement and is thus a disincentive to the improvement of children's education.

In its most serious form, the disincentives issue could be phrased in terms of a problem of "cheating." That is, schools might be tempted to suppress or tamper with test scores in order to lower the level of achievement and ensure continued funding. In its milder and more common form, the disincentives issue can be phrased in terms of a loss of morale or motivation at the level of the classroom, the school, or the school district. Personnel may find it discouraging to lose resources as a "reward" for improving achievement. Most teachers, principals, and administrators would argue that moving a school's average achievement score from the 35th to the 37th percentile, while no small victory, does not mean that the students in the school no longer need compensatory services. Yet if the cutoff is the 36th percentile, such an improvement may result in the loss of resources needed to continue providing special help for these children.

The two demonstration districts which chose to use achievement-based allocation—Winston-Salem and Charlotte—were perhaps more sensitive to the disincentives issue than the other districts. However, both succeeded in avoiding the problem. In the case of Winston-Salem, administrators chose to hold harmless the schools to be served during the demonstration. Making use of a kind of grandfather clause, they continued to serve some schools that would not have qualified by achievement criteria, because they believed that large-scale changes were excessively disturbing to the structure of their programs. In Charlotte, where there actually were large-scale changes in the number of schools served, some negative feelings were expressed, by principals whose schools lost services. The district administrators countered by pointing out that the implementation phase of the demonstration was only two years and that services would in all likelihood be restored.

While we could not examine the disincentives issue directly, the demonstration did provide an opportunity to gather opinions on this issue from local Title I personnel and school administrators. In virtually all the districts in which administrators were asked about the possibility of disincentives, the problem was regarded as one which was or could be offset by positive incentives. They pointed out that improving achievement is so basic a part of educational philosophy that it was unlikely that educators could be tempted to do otherwise. They mentioned more specific offsetting incentives as well. The two North Carolina districts felt that the state and local emphasis on improving reading achevement was so strong (reading achievement had been an issue in the last gubernatorial election) that is outweighed any potential disincentives.

Competing incentives were perhaps most concrete in Houston, where the state department of education has developed a stringent accountability policy that ties teacher and principal salaries and job security to student achievement. California has also taken steps to counteract potential disincentives. The Achievement Growth Incentive Plan is part of the state's policy of rewarding successful early childhood education programs with additional funds for expansion. Under the Achievement Growth Incentive Plan, which operated in Alum Rock during both years of the demonstration, additional funds are awarded to those ten schools in which students achieve the greatest growth, as measured by reading scores on standard achievement tests.

The issue of disincentives was not directly faced or defused as a political concern by the demonstration. Nevertheless, it appears that the demonstration districts, and probably most school districts, believe that offsetting incentives either exist or can be devised to deal with the problem. On its face, this theory appears to be quite reasonable. However, given the final shape of the 1978 Amendments (see postscript), it seems unlikely that it will be tested in the near future.

PARENT INVOLVEMENT

The role extended to Title I parents by federal legislation has been expanding since the original passage of Title I in 1965. In 1966 Congress required local school districts to consult community action agencies established by the Economic Opportunity Act about the planning, development, and operation of programs. But school districts were not legally required to involve parents of Title I students until 1971. That year the Commissioner of Education ordered each school system with a Title I program to establish an advisory council with Title I parents on it. In the Education Amendments of 1974 Congress strengthened the parent involvement provisions of Title I by requiring an advisory council at each school.

The strengthening of the parent role has not been accompanied by a clarification of purpose. As Hill points out, "At different times, PACs [parent advisory councils] are presented as ways to encourage parents to take greater interest in their children's education; as ways of incorporating parents' special wisdom into the planning of instruction; as generalized accountability devices for all LEA [local educational agency] policy; as possible foci for more general community action efforts [and] as ways of providing a local source of attention to faithful implementation of the program's objectives."[3] McLaughlin et al. classify these diverse roles into two basic types: the parent participation model and the parent-training model.[4] The parent participation model includes the parent-as-learner role (information sharing, parent workshops), the volunteer or untrained school worker role, and the governance role. The parent-training model is based on the parent as teacher—either facilitator or tutor.

The 1974 Amendments attempted to strengthen the parent role by encouraging greater parent participation in the area of governance. With the required establishment of school-level in addition to district-level parent advisory councils, parents were expected to play a role in program design, implementation, and monitoring. In Hill's terms, they were to be concerned with "generalized accountability" and community action, as well as a source of attention to faithful implementation of federal purpose.

This set of governance roles, although seldom exercised, could be a major source of pressure for compliance with the objectives of Title I. Indeed, Murphy suggests that the federal government has no real power to implement its policies.[5] According to Murphy, federal officials share with poor parents the distinction of being outside the nation's school system. He further states that federal interests and the interests of the poor could be well served if the two worked together as a countervailing force to the system of professional educators, which may be presumed to have a different set of interests.[6] Indeed, certain advocacy groups exhort district and local parent advisory groups to pursue this tack—to play the watchdog role at the local level. *Title I in Your Community,* a handbook for parents of Title I children prepared by the NAACP Legal Defense Fund, expresses disappointment with the history of Title I:

> Title I has not always provided the benefits and opportunities for better education that had been expected when the legislation was passed in 1965. The program was implemented on a crash basis and, in the first few years, school districts had few guidelines on how to spend the money. Most spent it in any way they wished without regard to the needs of poor children. Many financially hard-pressed school districts have simply spent the money on the needs of the entire system or group

of schools, or have spent Title I funds on services for poor children that other children in the system were already getting out of the regular budget.[7]

The handbook goes on to say that regulations have been written to involve poor parents in Title I programs but that most districts have ignored or violated them. However, the authors see some hope:

> There has also been an increasing demand by alert individuals and community organizations that Title I funds be spent on the most pressing educational needs of children and that there be genuine parental involvement. Parents in districts in all parts of the country have begun to monitor the use of funds, to establish parent councils, to file complaints with the Department of Health, Education and Welfare, and to file lawsuits in federal courts.[8]

In the 1974 Amendments mandating the demonstration, power was given to parents to disapprove allocation changes and therefore to veto participation in the demonstration if they wished. The passage reads, "Not more than twenty local educational agencies may elect *with the approval of the district-wide parent advisory council* ... to allocate funds ... on the basis of a method or combination of methods other than the method provided under Section 141(A)" (emphasis added).[9] Some in Congress feared (others hoped) that parent reaction to proposed district changes would scuttle attempts at radical modification of Title I distribution procedures. Thus, while the demonstration was not primarily a study of parent involvement, it did provide a unique opportunity to view the manner in which parents can exercise their authority with respect to program design and implementation.

The requirement that the parent advisory councils be involved in planning of the local demonstration projects further allowed us to see to what degree districts would actually open their educational planning process to parents, and how parents would respond. We used an adapted form of Arnstein's ladder of participation in an attempt to determine what decision-making power was actually afforded to parent advisory councils during that year.[10] This device allowed us to array participants on a continuum ranging from minimal participation (such as receiving information) to core planning group (those who decide what is to be done).

In none of the districts were the parent advisory councils part of the core planning group which formulated alternative policies, explored their implications for which schools and students would be served, and designed implementation strategies. That group tended to be composed of Title I and other district administrative personnel. However, in three of the districts the parent advisory council held a partnership with the core planning group, providing input into the decisions being made.

Of those three districts, Santa Fe illustrates best the role parents can play as partners in educational governance. While the basic strategy for reallocation of Title I resources in Santa Fe was made by a core planning group comprised of professional educators, parents were involved in a number of policy committees which met frequently to review the program and discuss alternative methods of providing services. As a result of this participation, the parent advisory council agreed to expand services from eleven to all sixteen elementary schools in the district, provided an important stipulation was added to the final implementation plan. To ensure that the demonstration would not dilute services to the current Title I population, parents insisted that the costs for expanding the program to newly eligible Title I schools not exceed the monies available from the use of carry-over funds or an increase in Title I allocation.

Adams County #12, where the planning process was also open to parents, provides a somewhat different example of parents in partnership. In this district the parent advisory council turned over to the Title I program the funds allotted to the council so that the money could be used for educational services. The council supported itself through a number of fund-raising activities, such as bake sales.

The dramatic use of parent power in Wichita illustrates both the potential influence of parent councils inherent in the federal legal framework and the fear of parents which may be felt by local administrators. One of the sixteen districts originally funded during the planning year, Wichita was forced by the district parent advisory council to withdraw from the demonstration.[11] The district's interest in the demonstration had been prompted by problems it was having providing Title I services following school desegregation.

In order to participate in the demonstration, interested districts were required to submit a proposal for the baseline (planning) year to NIE. Like the later proposal for implementation, the document had to be approved by the parent advisory council. Wichita's proposal was presented to the district council as the closing item on the agenda at a meeting in May 1975. The members expressed concern that implementing the proposal would mean that services would be diluted or some students presently receiving Title I services would lose them. The proposal was discussed again at the June meeting, and the same concerns were again raised.

After these two meetings, only the council chairperson was involved prior to submission of the proposal to NIE. She was asked to submit a letter with the proposal indicating council support of the plan. At the time she signed the letter, she had neither seen the completed proposal nor been informed of the parent advisory council's mandated participation. The proposal was submitted to and funded by NIE during the summer.

Council members were still unaware of the key role they were supposed to be playing during the planning year when they met with the districts's newly appointed demonstration project director the following October. They were concerned, however, when they saw the actual breakdown of services proposed. The major issue centered on the selection of schools, which seemed to favor schools in middle-class areas, and the distribution of services, which appeared to imply significant dilution. The parent advisory council formed a subcommittee to try to work with the district administrators on these problems.

At the end of October several Wichita council members attended a national conference of Title I parents and learned that in some areas the Wichita Title I program was not in compliance. First, the parent advisory council had not been involved in the demonstration planning to the extent required by the RFP. Second, although the district had been desegregated since 1971, target schools were still being selected on the basis of residential area rather than school enrollment. Finally, in some schools Title I and non-Title I students were receiving precisely the same corrective reading services. At the conference parents were advised by the Federal Education Project of the Lawyer's Committee for Civil Rights Under Law to pursue these concerns. On their return to Wichita, these parents maintained close contact with the Lawyers' Committee staff and requested that OE officials clarify the compliance issues.

At a November meeting of the council, an NIE project monitor stated that parent involvement in the project was mandatory. At his request, copies of the May 1975 proposal were made available to council members for the first time, and their involvement was officially accepted by the district administrators. However, although parents were promised opportunities for involvement in further planning efforts, they were given few.

The council became convinced that the district administrators would proceed to formulate implementation plans with as little involvement by parents as possible and then expect the council to vote its approval without a clear understanding of what they were voting for. As early as November, 1975, district council members voted not to approve or disapprove of the demonstration plan unless they had the full proposal in hand and guarantees that no changes would be made after their decision was made. The matter was put to a vote in April 1976 at the insistence of project personnel. In discussion previous to the actual vote, several issues were raised but not resolved; foremost among these was the possible dilution of services. Believing themselves to be better off with Title I in its current form and convinced that their concerns were not being addressed, the parent advisory council voted twelve to five against implementation of the demonstration project.

The Wichita story illustrates several elements which have been mentioned previously. First, parents must understand how to use the legal framework to exercise their influence. In the case of Wichita the Federal Education Project of the Lawyers' Committee for Civil Rights Under Law advised the council of its rights. Second, the linkage between the parent advisory council and federal agencies (in this case OE and NIE) facilitates the functioning of the council as a grassroots constituency for Title I. Third, parents can apply pressure to a school district by raising such technical issues as dilution of services and supplanting. The Wichita parent advisory council demanded answers rather than reassurances from the district educators and refused to acquiesce when they decided the answers were unsatisfactory.

Many educational administrators would see the amount of influence wielded by parents in Wichita as excessive, and it is not surprising that local administrators in Wichita took a dim view of the council's action. From the district's point of view, the parent advisory council's failure to support the demonstration was based on ignorance concerning the proposed changes, and both the school board and the newspapers presented it that way. The board interpreted the council's veto as the minority view of a selfish few, who through lack of understanding sought to limit the Wichita program for the disadvantaged.

Both educators and parents in Wichita believed they had the best interests of the Title I program at heart. However, they had different agendas. The educational establishment in Wichita, as in many of the demonstration districts, was interested in expanding services. The parents wanted to protect services for the population of children they represented. While Santa Fe succeeded in channeling these competing interests into a compromise strategy, Wichita did not.

The recognition that parent advisory councils and district educational administrators are likely to have differing agendas should lead to some clarification of the regulations at the federal level. The wording of the demonstration mandate giving parents veto power over the demonstration is unique within Title I. Which role is it that the federal government wishes parents to play? If it is that of local watchdog, then the current system must spell out the terms of the relationship in greater detail. Most of the workings of the district-parent relationship are now defined at the local level. The council must either take the initiative in playing a governance role or be given that role by the district administrators, who may be reluctant to grant it. As Wichita illustrates, such a role can be very powerful.

CONCLUSION

The demonstration helped lay to rest three myths which have surrounded proposed changes in the Title I legal framework. First, increased local autonomy, when coupled with state and federal oversight, does not necessarily lead to abuse of Title I funds. Under careful scrutiny, the relaxation of federal rules governing allocation of Title I dollars and the coordination of Title I and other compensatory education funds can lead to innovative and sound mechanisms for program delivery. Also, the simple opportunity to reexamine current delivery patterns may result in a challenge to overly restrictive interpretations of federal regulations and the more efficient and integrated use of all available resources.

Second, although determining school eligibility on the basis of achievement may bring about disincentives for school administrators and teachers, there are several mechanisms and countervailing forces which reduce the problem. Existing hold-harmless provisions can soften the impact of changes in school achievement on changes in eligibility status. In addition, state and local funds can be used, within limits, as competing incentives for schools to improve achievement. Furthermore, professional pride, coupled with accountability requirements, can counter any disincentive to improve student performance.

Finally, we have seen that parents who fully understand their rights can wield considerable influence. If granted a legitimate governance role, they are capable of grasping complex and technical issues and making decisions in tandem with professional educators. On the other hand, if thwarted, they can use their considerable power to negate local initiatives when those initiatives and their own interests appear to diverge.

Notes

1.   The data which form the basis of this discussion are taken primarily from on-site interviews with personnel involved in the local Title I demonstration projects. These interviews are augmented by the statements of district personnel made at a November, 1977, site conference sponsored by NIE in Washington, D.C., and by written answers supplied to questions asked of the districts in the spring of 1978. Interviews with Title I and non-Title I parents in 1976 and 1977 serve as the data source for much of the discussion of parent involvement, with additional information drawn from reports submitted to Abt Associates by the district research coordinators (local residents hired to facilitate district data collection).

2.   Murphy, "Title I of ESEA"; and Hill, "Enforcement and Informal Pressure."

3.   Hill, "Enforcement and Informal Pressure," p. 32.

4.   McLaughlin et al., *The Effects of Title I, ESEA.*

5.   Murphy, "Title I of ESEA."

6.   This group of interests is represented by personnel employed by the state or local educational agency. As Hill points out, state- or local-level Title I personnel are more affiliated with the program and represent another Title I constituency.

7.   NAACP, *Title I in Your Community,* p. i.

8.   Ibid.

9.   Title I Statute, Section 150a.

10. Sherry R. Arnstein, "A Ladder of Citizen Participation," *American Institute of Planners Journal* (July 1969): 216-224.

11. Two other districts also dropped out of the demonstration after the planning year; however, their reasons for doing so were largely unrelated to parent pressure.

Postscript

= Postscript =

More than four years after the passage of the Education Amendments of 1974, President Jimmy Carter sat down at a small table in the State Dining Room of the White House and, under the watchful eyes of nearly 150 invited guests, signed the Education Amendments of 1978 into law. In 1974 few would have predicted that Title I would be subject to so many major changes. However, in terms of program operation, the 1978 act represents the most important set of alterations since Title I was first enacted in 1965.

The 1978 amendments were profoundly influenced by the findings of the NIE Compensatory Education Study, including the demonstration results. The study is described in the House Report as the "first comprehensive evaluation of Title I since its enactment."[1]

In contrast to the changes made in 1974, which largely affected the manner in which Title I funds were allocated to districts, the changes made in 1978 influence the manner in which funds are allocated within districts, as well as affecting the design and implementation of local Title I programs, and the coordination of Title I with other compensatory education programs. In general, these changes are designed to permit districts greater flexibility in determining school eligibility, to remove unintended negative effects of federal laws and regulations on state compensatory education programs, and to respond to specific concerns about the equitable distribution of resources. While some of the changes represent new initiatives, others are intended to codify or clarify existing OE regulations and policy interpretations—an indication that Congress took seriously the finding that the Title I legal framework lacked sufficient clarity. Some changes in the law were designed to legitimize actual practice.

Several amendments can be traced either directly or indirectly to the demonstration study and the issues raised earlier in this book. One such change is the dual ranking provision for determining school eligibility. In the past, only schools which had large concentrations of low-income students could be considered eligible. The Education Amendments of 1978 permit school districts which have gained the consent of the district parent advisory council and the state educational agency to rank schools according to both poverty and educational deprivation and then substitute schools with greater educational deprivation for those with greater poverty but less education deprivation. In order to prevent funds from being spread too thinly, the legislation states that a district may not designate a greater number of schools eligible for Title I services under this option than if it had not been used.

The dual ranking of schools reflects Representative Quie's concern that the most educationally deprived children may not attend schools with the highest poverty ranking. This was, of course, the original impetus for the demonstration study. With the enactment of the dual ranking provision, Congress sanctioned, for the first time, the use of educational deprivation as a legitimate basis for determination of school eligibility. It remains to be seen if this change in the direction of the program will be maintained or extended in 1983 when Title I is next reauthorized.

A second important change concerns the manner in which Title I funds may be allocated among schools within a given district. Both the NIE national survey and the demonstration study revealed that districts utilized numerous procedures for allocating funds among schools. As a result, the amount of instructional services received by Title I students could vary greatly depending on the school attended. The new amendment essentially ties the distribution of funds to the number and needs of students, as determined by educational criteria.

Beyond these substantive changes in the way Title I schools are designated and funds are allocated among them, the 1978 amendments include many changes which affect the way Title I dollars are used to provide services once they reach the school. By their very nature, these amendments affect many more districts than provisions relating to funds allocation and school designation.

For many districts and individual Title I schools the most important service-related amendment provides that any school enrolling 75 percent or more poor children may use Title I funds to conduct schoolwide projects. This provision addresses the fact that schools with large concentrations of low-income students find it difficult to separate non-Title I and Title I students. Furthermore, delivering services becomes problematic if, in a class of thirty children, twenty-seven are eligible for services, and adherence to the letter of the law means denying services to a fraction of the children in the classroom. The "schoolwide project" provision may be an example of the law mimicking actual practice. Certainly, the allocation choices made by at least two of the demonstration districts—Alum Rock and Yonkers—relected a preference for this option. Both districts have schools with high concentrations of educationally disadvantaged students.

This provision also addresses concern over the use of pullout instruction as a means for ensuring fiscal accountability. By deeming all students eligible for service in schools with large concentrations of low-income students, local administrators need not worry about reserving Title I-funded staff, materials, and/or equipment exclusively for Title I students.

It should be pointed out, however, that this schoolwide project provision has an important caveat. Title I per-pupil expenditures for educationally deprived children in schools with large concentrations of low-income children must equal per-pupil expenditures for educationally deprived children attending Title I schools with smaller concentrations of low-income children. Thus, supplementary state and local funds must be used to serve children who are not educationally deprived but who attend schools which involve the schoolwide project provision.

Finally, Congress modified several federal requirements concerning coordination of Title I with state and local compensatory funds. These changes were intended to assure Title I children a fair share of state and local compensatory funds without favoring them. The changes were also intended to discourage the overly restrictive interpretations of the rules adopted by many states and districts, to provide additional incentives for the expansion of special state and local programs, and to remove unnecessary barriers to program co-ordination.

First, the 1978 Amendments clarify the purpose of the supplanting provisions and broaden the frame of reference for considering whether Title I funds have supplanted special state and local funds. Consistent with OE's interpretation, the new statute specifies that all children *eligible* for Title I (rather than all children *participating* in Title I programs), are to be considered in determining whether supplanting has occurred. This modification was designed to ensure that all eligible children receive compensatory services, rather than that additional services be delivered to Title I students whose needs are already being met.

Second, the 1978 Amendments qualify the circumstances under which a district may tailor the distribution of state and local funds to the availability of Title I monies. In general, special state and local funds must be distributed according to state or local law without considering the availability of Title I funds. However, the new law states that the existence of Title I funds may be taken into account if the state or district employs objective criteria in determining which children will receive assistance under these funds and then follows seven steps prescribed by the statute. These steps are designed to ensure that state and local compensatory education funds are distributed without discrimination against Title I schools and children and at the same time permit coordinated planning and joint distribution of Title I and other compensatory funds. Essentially, the amendments clarify and extend the fair share provisions.

In order to encourage the expansion of state and local compensatory and other special programs, the new law also allows two additional exemptions from the comparability and excess cost provisions. The first exemption, which is identical to that already available for state and local compensatory education programs, concerns special state programs which are innovative but not compensatory in nature. Under certain circumstances, this provision exempts such programs from the comparability provision.

The legislation also creates a limited exemption from the supplement-not-supplant requirement in cases where state and local compensatory education funds are sizable. That is, if the amount of state or local funds used in Title I-eligible schools is equal to or greater than the amount of funds a district would have received had it received its full Title I authorization, the district may use additional state and local compensatory funds exclusively in non-Title I schools until these monies are brought up to the level of total compensatory funding (from any source) per program participant in Title I schools. Addressing an issue raised in chapter nine, this latter exemption allows state and local compensatory education monies to be used to serve children in need, regardless of school attendance area.

The study commissioned by NIE on the effects of using alternative allocation formulae for Title I of ESEA had its most pronounced immediate impact on the 1978 reauthorization of Title I. However, its influence has spread far beyond the legislative process. Because of changes which were incorporated in the 1978 amendments, the study was a valuable tool for the Office of Education to use in the preparation of regulations stemming from the legislation. It is also being used to assist in preparing the Title I policy manual mandated by Congress in Section 187 of the law.

Representative Albert Quie, who provided the impetus for the study and the changes in the law, departed from the Congress when he was elected Governor of Minnesota in November 1978. However, it is quite likely that the momentum established by the 1978 Quie amendments will result in further consideration of the appropriate beneficiaries of Title I. At the very least, the Congress will be forced to examine the pertinent policy issues again in the next reauthorization cycle if only to determine what impact the 1978 amendments have had on the allocation of resources and whether or not school districts have exercised any of the options available to them under the new law.

Other issues will certainly emerge in the course of the three years before the next reauthorization. One of the first may be in connection with proposals by the Carter administration to deal, at least in part, with high rates of youth unemployment by channeling compensatory education funds into the high schools via Title I. Another issue will be the effectiveness of Title I in promoting gains in student achievement. However, the biggest issues in 1982 and 1983 will center around data from the 1980 Census and the impact of that data on the reallocation of Title I resources among school districts. As in 1974, it is likely that all other concerns will pale in comparison, no matter how intriguing, intellectually rewarding, or compelling.

Notes

1. *Report on the Education Amendments of 1978,* p. 5.

ADDITIONAL READING

Readers who would like more detail about technical aspects of the Abt Associates demonstration study or more data on specific topics are referred to the volumes listed below. All are available through Abt Publications, 55 Wheeler Street, Cambridge, Massachusetts 02138.

Vanecko, James J., Archambault, Francis X., Jr., and Ames, Nancy L. *ESEA Title I Allocation Policy Demonstration Study: Implementation Decisions and Research Plan.* Cambridge, Mass.: Abt Associates Inc., 1976.

This volume presents an overview of the demonstration study, including the legislative mandate which provided its impetus, the issues surrounding the research design, and a description of the participating school districts. A detailed discussion of the allocation process is included with particular focus on the intradistrict allocation choices made by the thirteen demonstration districts before and after the granting of waivers from standard rules. The volume also contains an extensive discussion of the study and sample design.

Vanecko, James J., Archambault, Francis X., Jr., and Ames, Nancy L. *ESEA Title I Allocation Policy Demonstration Study: Analysis of Baseline Data* (vols. I and II). Cambridge, Mass.: Abt Associates Inc., October 31, 1977.

These two volumes present detailed data on the characteristics of and services received by Title I students in the thirteen demonstration districts prior to changing their allocation policies. The volume also describes the context for the demonstration, including the manner in which parents and educators interacted during the planning process. Detailed information on parent participation in other phases of the Title I program is also provided.

Vanecko, James J. et al. *ESEA Title I Allocation Policy Demonstration Study: Results of First Year Implementation* (vols. I and II). Cambridge, Mass.: Abt Associates Inc., March 30, 1978.

These volumes describe more fully demonstration-related changes in schools and students served, student characteristics and services, program delivery patterns, and the costs associated with such changes. The appendix to volume I includes the statement of James J. Vanecko before the Subcommittee on Elementary, Secondary, and Vocational Education of the U.S. House of Representatives.

Sjogren, Jane Huseby and Ames, Richard. *ESEA Title I Allocation Policy Demonstration Study: Cost Analysis, Planning Year 1975-76.* Cambridge, Mass.: Abt Associates Inc., September 1978.

This report describes resource uses and program costs of the Title I programs in the thirteen demonstration districts prior to the receipt of waivers from standard rules.

Index

Index

201

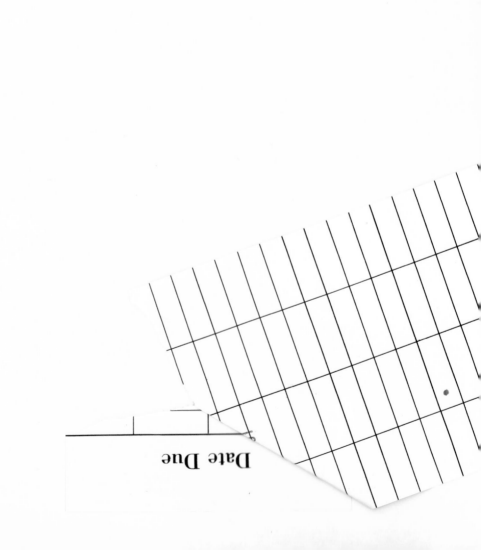

Date Due